INDIVIDUALIZING INSTRUCTION:
A COMPLETE GUIDE FOR
DIAGNOSIS, PLANNING,
TEACHING AND EVALUATION

Other Books by the Authors

Discipline and the Disruptive Child: A Practical Guide for Elementary Teachers

The Effective Student Activities Program

Experiential Learning: An Effective Teaching Program for Elementary Schools

Successful Methods for Teaching the Slow Learner

INDIVIDUALIZING INSTRUCTION: A COMPLETE GUIDE FOR DIAGNOSIS, PLANNING, TEACHING AND EVALUATION

Muriel Schoenbrun Karlin

Regina Berger

PARKER PUBLISHING COMPANY, INC.

WEST NYACK, N.Y.

Library of Congress Cataloging in Publication Data

Karlin, Muriel Schoenbrun.
   Individualizing instruction.

    1. Individualized instruction. I. Berger,
Regina, joint author. II. Title.
LB1031.K37   372.1'39'4   73-15846
ISBN 0-13-457507-5

Printed in the United States of America

DEDICATION

We dedicate this book to the intellectually needy child, and to his or her parents and teachers, with the hope it will be of value in shedding light where light so often has been denied.

How this book will
help you, the teacher. . . .

Today, a great deal of attention is being focused on the education of each child. In previous years, there has never been as much emphasis placed on the instruction of the individual as there is now. As we move into this era, our concern as educators is to teach every boy and girl in terms of his or her own unique needs and abilities. Instruction, in effect, is becoming more personalized, in order to make it more effective. The purpose of this book is to enable you to do this with *your* youngsters, in *your* classroom. It is a realistic guide to the various steps you must take to make learning truly meaningful for each one of your students—the slow, the average and the bright child.

Before we can begin to teach a child, we must know exactly what material he has mastered in any given area. This is particularly true of individual skills—whether in reading comprehension, or in arithmetic, science or social studies. It is far easier to teach a child how to structure a sentence correctly than to let him repeatedly write "run-ons," but first you must realize that he really doesn't understand the concept of the complete sentence. You must diagnose constantly—to find the needs of the individual child. For it is entirely possible that, while Johnny may not know what a sentence really is, little Mary does—and what a waste of time it is to teach it to her repeatedly. Many pages of this book are devoted to helping you diagnose the needs of every child—in terms of what he has learned—and what he hasn't.

In addition to these academic needs, his needs as a human being are discussed—the need to achieve, to be accepted, to develop feelings of self-confidence and of being wanted. We consider these needs because their fulfillment is so important if the child is to function well, both in school, now, and in the career world of his future.

After diagnosis, we will proceed to lesson planning. There will be some new material you will be presenting to the entire class, and for this a traditional plan is effective. However, much of your material will need to be individualized. You will find how to plan for both types of instruction. In the skills areas, individual goals are necessary for every child. We will show you how to establish them. Your planning, based, of course, on your diagnosis of the child's needs, is the key to your success.

Following this is a section on teaching techniques—what to do when you are actually working with the children. It contains ideas for you in every subject area. It begins with chapters on structuring the classroom to make individualized instruction possible, and to give you the time for it. You will find actual descriptions of teaching situations, and suggestions for making them most effective. Suggestions are given for devices you can use—textbooks, worksheets, filmstrips, programmed learning. Teacher-made materials are even more important and they are described in detail.

Because you will find there are usually a number of children who have similar needs in any one class, techniques for grouping are covered. For the same reason, team teaching is discussed, in an informal as well as a formal structure.

Unless evaluation is an important part of your teaching process, you cannot know how successful your efforts have been. It must be a continuing, essential part of every unit of work. Tests, to have the greatest value, should be used as diagnostic tools as well. The traditional ideas of the pre-test, and the final test of a unit are sound—if both are used to show us what material the child has not learned—so that we can then teach it to him.

Throughout the book, emphasis is placed on teaching the individual child, and on his intellectual development. By this individualization of instruction, we help the child who is unable to divide, *and* the student who is ready to study calculus. It is a necessity if we are to reach this generation of youngsters,whose education comes from so many sources. Individualized instruction is an effective way of making the teacher indispensable, for it emphasizes the human element of teaching as well as the technical. It enables us to bring out the very best in every child—and in ourselves, as teachers.

M.S.K.
R.B.

ACKNOWLEDGMENTS

Among the many persons to whom we are indebted for their cooperation in the preparation of this manuscript, we wish to thank particularly the following:

> Mr. Maurice Wollin, Community Superintendent, District 31, Staten Island, New York.
> Mrs. Helen Harris, Educational and Vocational Counselor, Public School 82, Manhattan.
> Mr. Norman H. Harris, Principal, Anning S. Prall Intermediate School, Staten Island, New York

Many photographs were supplied by the Office of Education Information Services and Public Relations, Board of Education, City of New York. Superintendent Jerome G. Kovalcik has been most helpful, and we wish to publicly thank photographers John Kane and John Fulner.

Mr. Les Trautmann, Editor of the Staten Island Advance, generously provided several excellent photos which had appeared in that publication, and which were taken by Mr. Barry Schwartz.

Special honorable mention is also due to Roberta Schoenbrun (Mrs. Arnold Schoenbrun) of the Oceanside School District. She enriched our book with her contract in the Science Chapter, and other contributions throughout. Her verve and enthusiasm for individualized instructions reverberate in these pages.

Our appreciation, too, to our typist, Irene Weiss (Mrs. Henry Weiss) of Cedarhurst, Long Island, whose painstaking efforts in our behalf are deeply appreciated. The long and arduous task of proofreading was done by Dr. Leonard Karlin, by Mr. Henry Karlin and Miss Lisa Karlin. Many of our colleagues whose names are not mentioned, have furnished excellent ideas which we have recorded in these pages.

Contents

How this book will help you, the teacher 7

1. Diagnostic testing for the individual instruction program 17

    Key factors in individualized instruction   17
    Individualized instruction is for the bright child as well
    as the slow and average child   18
    Skills and subject matter   20
    Determining the child's needs   21
    Assign priorities   22
    Guidelines for developing your own diagnostic tests   22
    Motivating the children   24
    Informal diagnosis by examination of written work   24
    How to make the results of your diagnostic tests work   25
    Grouping children with similar needs   26
    Motivation: showing the child he can learn   27
    Teaching responsibility   29

2. Establishing goals and planning lessons that individualize
instruction 30

    Goals for every child   33
    Using the conventional lesson plan   36
    Unit plans make individualization easier   37
    Unit plans make individualization easier   37
    Using a planbook or index cards   38
    A sample unit for the second grade   39
    Using the story to the fullest extent   42
    The contract   43
    Taking into consideration the differing rates of learning   44
    Using a variety of approaches   44
    Keeping your planning flexible   45
    Using your plans as a record for future reference   46

3.   Measuring the basic psychological needs of each child **48**

The basic psychological needs of every child   48
Why every child needs to build a positive self-image
and how individualized instruction can foster this   48
How can you get this?   49
Giving every child responsibilities   50
The need for a physically beautiful environment,
created and maintained by the children   52
Developing self-pride—"We write our own price tags"   52
Caring for living things   53
Developing feelings of accomplishment   54
Rewards for accomplishment   55
Rewards   56
Occasions for a party   56
Trips   57
Individualized trips   58
Individualized commendation cards   58
Commendation letters   58
Defeating the defeatist attitude   59
Confidentially   60
Individualized instruction for the sick child   61

4.   How to make time for individualized instruction 64

Established routines   64
Entering the classroom   66
Seating arrangements   67
Hanging up clothing   68
Keeping the room clean   68
Individualized responsibility   69
Rules for individualized responsibility   69
How can you get this to function well?   71
Routines which save your time and that of the children   71
Explain the system of individualized instruction and how
it works   72
Teaching children to teach other children   74
Research and group work   74
Building a success pattern for every child   76
Team teaching   77

5. **Teaching self-control—the essential ingredient for a successful individualized program**..................................... **79**

Having the children establish rules   79
Distributing copies of the rules   81
Making children familiar with school regulations   82
Using the school handbook   82
Establish rewards and penalties   83
Establishing class teams   85
Class officers   85
Working privately with the children who have problems   86
Trips   87

6. **The key to teaching every child to read—by individualizing instruction** **90**

Diagnosing progress in vocabulary development   91
Diagnosing progress in reading comprehension   93
Working on reading, skill by skill   95
Configuration clues   96
Phonetic analysis   98
Games with phonics   99
Structural analysis   100
Contextual clues   101
Teaching reading comprehension   102
Teaching each child, or grouping those with similar needs   104
Assigning reading gives you time to work
with each child   105
Making reading a pleasure   107
Reading races   108

7. **Teaching the language arts skills every child must have** **110**

Establishing goals   110
How to teach the use of our language   111
How can you teach these skills, and reach these
objectives?   113
Grammar as a living force   113
Spelling, capitalization and punctuation   115
Spelling   116

7. Teaching the language arts skills every child must have (*continued*)

Capitalization and punctuation   117
Developing diagnostic tests in written language   118
Finding time for individualized instructions   119
Individualizing instruction by bringing out the children's talents   120
How to work on specific skill areas   122
Parental aid   123
Teaching the art of sentence structuring   123
Working toward more descriptive writing   123
Vocabulary games for individualizing instructions   124
Some children need to learn to express themselves verbally   125
Learning the art of listening   126
Teaching handwriting, the almost forgotten art   127
Enrichment for the brighter children   132

8. Making sure no child is an arithmetic dropout **135**

Arithmetic, a house of cards   135
Diagnostic tests for every skill   136
Discovering the child's inadequacies   137
Teaching the curriculum and the skill areas   138
For the children who don't need remediation   140
Combating carelessness, the big enemy   141
Helping children to learn the steps in problem solving   142
Teaching the reading skills the child needs to succeed in arithmetic   143
The vocabulary of arithmetic   144
Helping the bright child to forge ahead   145
Games to make arithmetic fun   146
The arithmetic laboratory   147

9. Developing more meaningful experiences in social studies through individualization **149**

Determining the child's ability to handle social studies skills   151
Handling the curriculum   153
Reading in the social studies area   154
Teaching the vocabulary of social studies   155

9. **Developing more meaningful experiences in social studies through individualization** (*continued*)

> Debates and panel discussions, and helping each child prepare for them 156
> Individualizing instruction in regard to social attitudes 157
> Bringing the child and television together intelligently 159
> Teaching children critical thinking 160
> Teaching children how to read news reports in both newspapers and magazines . . . with a grain of salt! 161
> Committee work to teach the children how to work with others 161
> Trips 164

10. **How individualized instruction can improve your science teaching. . 167**

> Experiments for each child 170
> The scientific method 173
> Individualizing the curriculum 174
> Find texts which each child can read and understand 177
> A science problem which enables you to work with every child individually 177
> Children may work with each other 179
> Building an interest in ecology 179
> Make each child responsible for a living thing in the classroom 180
> What are you going to be when you grow up? 181
> Survival lessons 182
> Narcotics, alcohol and cigarette smoking 182

11. **Individualizing instruction to foster creativity in art, music, home economics, industrial arts and health education 185**

> Encouraging each child to explore his talents 186
> Giving each child to explore his talents 188
> Giving each child a jumping-off place 188
> Sampling new ideas 190
> What to do to start off the child who feels he has no talent 191
> Avoiding negative criticism 192

11. **Individualizing instruction to foster creativity in art, music, home economics, industrial arts and health education** (*continued*)

For talent to flourish, sincere encouragement is
the keynote   193
Introducing the world of art and music to your children   195
Opening the youngsters' eyes to the wonder of the world
around them   197
How to teach, even if you are not particularly talented
in any of these areas   197

12. **Individualization of instruction in teaching children
work and behavior skills** **201**

Teaching a child how to study   202
How to study guide   203
How to learn from a text   205
Using the study methods   205
Reviewing in class   205
Specific teaching for testing   206
How to study for any test   207
Teaching children social behavior in this changing
world   208
A questionnaire on social attitudes   208
Giving children experiences in getting along together   211
Developing rapport with the disruptive child   212

13. **Evaluating your success with individualized instruction** **214**

Evaluation should be a constant process   214
Pretesting before initiating individualized instruction   216
End of unit tests are diagnostic tests, too   218
Varying and individualizing the types of tests you give—
oral, open book, essay and short-answer   219
Teaching every child the technique for answering essay
questions   221
Allowing the class to grade its own tests   222
Reviewing the test results and using them for
individualization   223
Building a success pattern with testing   224

13. Evaluating your success with individualized instruction (*continued*)

Keep a file of your tests   226
Evaluating individual growth in social behavior   227
Conclusion   229

Index 231

1

Diagnostic testing for the individualized instruction program

Key factors in individualized instruction

Individualized instruction is certainly not a new idea. Good teachers have been doing it since classrooms and schools were invented. Each time you walk around the room, and stop to help a child, are you not individualizing instruction? Every time you suggest to a child, "If you liked *Born Free,* read *The Yearling.* You'll love it," you are working with an individual. Today, however, emphasis is being placed on educating each and every youngster, and on getting him to assume responsibility for his behavior. There are many facets in this program which you will find covered in these pages, but underlying them all are these basic concepts:

1. Our fundamental task, as educators, is to create in the child the desire to learn, and to develop in him a real thirst for knowledge, so that a desire for education will motivate and enrich his entire life. By individualizing instruction, we are better able to reach every child, affect every child's life and get every child actively participating in the educational process.

2. It is never too early to begin individualizing instruction. In fact, the need for it is far greater in the primary grades than later

on. This is important for the same reason that the foundation of a house is important. By individualizing instruction, we can make sure the educational foundation, the framework, the basis of all that comes after, is not faulty. The lack of an adequate foundation, we believe, has been the greatest failure of education. It seems monstrous that we have left some children standing at the post, while others, even their own classmates, speed off. What humiliation the slower child must endure! What destructive mechanisms can come into being when a child feels that he is less adequate than the others who sit beside him, day in, day out, and who are making progress.

Our influence, as teachers, in the lower grades is far more pronounced than when the children become older. The close contact the child has with the teacher during the period of individualized instruction enables the youngster to relate to an adult. It serves to mold his character, for at this time of his life the child is particularly pliable. He will lean with affection toward the teacher, especially in this one-to-one relationship. If the teacher is able to empathize, if she can really feel for the child, and understand him, much can be accomplished.

3. It is our task, too, to awaken an intellectual responsibility so that the child learns to shoulder it willingly—and even enjoy it. He must be shown it is up to him to learn so that he may enrich his own life and the lives of others.

4. Individualized instruction is based on diagnosis to determine the children's academic needs. If a child has grasped all of the material presented to him, he needs additional work. If he has not grasped the material, he needs reinforcement and new learning experiences, until he is able to learn it.

Individualized instruction is for the bright child as well as the slow and average child

Within your lifetimes, have you not seen our profession change and yet remain the same? At one time early in this century, there were actually 100 children in a class. Today, there are 30 to 35 youngsters in a class, and in some fortunate cases even fewer. Yet basically, the intent was the same then as it is now—to teach every child. The variations have entered in the manner in which we go about this. *For we must teach every child.* This is what our profession is all about. Not the average, not the slow, not the bright, but every child. To some extent we have been doing this, of course. But to some extent we have not, and this has been the root of many of the problems we face today. In writing this book, our goal is to help you to develop methods and techniques to reach and teach every child. The big difference is that we, and you, will be considering each one as an individual, gearing work to him and trying to peer into his mind to see if he really is learning. Our thinking must change. It is not the class, but the child.

Individualized instruction is not solely for the slow learner. It is for every child whom it is your task to teach. The slow learner, of late, has received a good deal of attention—and he is surely in need of this attention. He will receive much of it in the pages of this volume, too. Our book, *Successful Methods for Teaching the Slow Learner,* is geared to him, and to understanding his problems. He has become a national problem, stemming, of course, from social conditions. We know why he exists—but we, as teachers, cannot excuse or condone his lack of learning and we can, and must do something about it—by teaching him individually.

But what about his average classmate, who goes along learning a bit every now and then? What can we do to motivate him, to entice him, to cajole him to learn? First we must know where he is—what he has learned, and what he is learning. Then we can move him along. What is holding him back? How can we find out? This is what we shall help you with—almost immediately.

And now that bright child. Is he really making progress or is he reaching a stalemate? Moreover, is he getting bored? Is he finding far less stimulation in the classroom than in the world outside? Are you challenging him? We have very tough competition. We have to contend with television, for example, which does everything—and successfully entices the child's attention. It is one of the potentially best sources of education in the world. We have to contend with films, more outspoken in many areas than they have ever been. We have to contend with the stimuli in the newspapers and magazines—some good, some not so good. But, with such stimuli the school experience can be a relatively tame one by comparison. This is particularly true for the bright child; unless we can fire his imagination, and offer him stimuli as fascinating as those he meets outside—or even more so. And we can, for we have the wisdom of the ages at our disposal. We can, too, offer him a wealth of new experiences—not as a voyeur of television, but as a participant in life. Individualizing instruction is a tall order when we think of the number of children for whom it should be done—but it can stimulate each child—to think and to learn. It will bring you great rewards, if you will attempt it.

Skills and subject matter

In our thinking, it helps to divide individualized instruction into the skills area and the subject areas. When we do this we find a very interesting situation. There are many bright children who are sadly lacking in skills.

Class 7-XYZ is a class of intellectually gifted children. There are 32 boys and girls in this class, all of whose I.Q.s are over 125. They are bright and sparkling, yet when they were asked to write a short paragraph, commenting on a specific film they had been shown for this purpose, the results were as follows:

> 20 had run-on sentences.
> 18 made serious errors in spelling.
> 6 had little comprehension of what it means to write a paragraph.
> 30 had spelling errors.

These results are hardly out of the ordinary. Yet these are bright children, alert and attentive. They had been interested in the film, for it had been carefully selected for the exercise, but they had not learned many of the skills involved in writing paragraphs. They are highly verbal—excellent in discussion, but poor in writing. (One thinks of the future. If these youngsters have not learned to write a letter of application, how will they ever be able to apply for jobs, when that time comes?)

Our colleges are experiencing these phenomena. Some college students seem to have little command of written English.

The same holds true of arithmetic skills. As you proceed in your individualizing of instruction, you will find many children lacking in some of them. There will be skills they have not learned, and others they have forgotten.

The purpose of diagnostic testing which you will be using

throughout your teaching is especially important in regard to skills. It shows up the holes in the child's background—the specific areas he must learn if he is to progress.

In every subject, there are certain skill areas. In science, there is the use of the scientific method. In social studies, there are a variety of skills, such as map reading, dealing with chronology, being able to relate events to one another, cause and effect—all of these are involved in geography and history. And if we are really to teach social studies, should we not be teaching the children the skills they should use in order to get along with one another—the skills of social behavior?

Reading skills are probably of the greatest concern to the greatest number of people. Of course we must place tremendous emphasis on the ability to read. Again, every child must be able to read. Not 30 out of 32, but 32 out of 32. Every child. It is every child's birthright to be able to read. Once a child learns to read he can learn anything he wants to learn. Even a very bright child, who has a reading block and does not master the techniques of reading, will go through life seriously handicapped. This child will feel inferior as a result, and may develop anti-social traits if the right to read is denied him. We propose to help you teach him to read and to comprehend.

Determining the child's needs

In doing diagnostic testing, you will be able to determine exactly what areas the child needs to have emphasized. With the brighter child, these will be far fewer in number than with his slower classmate. When you have pinpointed the problems, you will then plan work geared to helping the child master them. Sometimes he will do this rather quickly, whereas at other times you will have to keep working on a specific area over and over again. For example, we mentioned run-on sentences. This seems to be one specific which is very difficult for the child to master. You can try to analyze why—does he understand the concept of a complete thought? As he gets more sophisticated, can he see how to join thoughts in one sentence—without it becoming run on? Still later on, can he comprehend the use of conjunctions? As you work with the child, analyze constantly to determine, if you can, the direction of his thinking in this one relatively limited area.

Assign priorities

When a child is deficient in many skills, it becomes necessary for you to assign priorities, and to work on those rather than spreading his attention too thin. If a child needs work on phonics, no matter what grade he is in, hit the topic of phonics—and hit it hard. (Of course you will use material appropriate to his age and interests. "Babyish" material would turn any child's attention away—indeed drive it away. But a child will learn "ph" in Philadelphia (where it appears twice) more quickly than in the word "phonics.")

Where a child is experiencing difficulty, you should, in your planning, find a variety of approaches. However, be sure you concentrate on this problem area; don't move merrily along because if you do the problem remains unsolved. As a child solves a problem, or masters a topic, be very sure he is aware of his success, for it is an absolute necessity that you build his self-confidence.

Guidelines for developing your own diagnostic tests

The basic tool in individualized instruction is diagnostic testing. There are many tests commercially available. However, you can easily compose your own. The following method will work in virtually any subject area.

1. In any grade but the first, we suggest you use either the textbooks or the curriculum of the previous grade. The textbook is generally easier to use.

2. At the beginning of the term, if you are doing diagnostic testing for grade 6 in math, for example, obtain several grade 5 textbooks. Use the questions, problems or exercises at the end of each chapter.

3. Select 5 to 10 sample questions from each chapter. Use both simple and difficult ones.

4. Be sure you include every topic the chapter covers.

5. Give this test to the children over a period of days.

6. Explain it is a diagnostic test to help them—and you—to discover in which topics they are weak.

7. If a child misses the simple questions, he needs a unit of work in that area.

8. If, *after redoing this unit,* he has not mastered it, go back to the text of the year before, and design another test.

It is essential you find out which building blocks are lacking in the child's education. This is one way in which you can do this.

9. If a child can handle the simple questions, but not the more complex, he, too, needs work in that area. Usually, however, it is not necessary to go back to the work of two years before.

10. Make sure that the questions are phrased so that the child can comprehend them.

Here we encounter that old bugaboo—reading. If a child cannot read, he will undoubtedly have difficulty with any test you give him. We have come around to it again; if a child cannot read, he will experience academic difficulty—over and over again. Even in arithmetic, if he cannot read a problem, how can he solve it?

Be sure your diagnostic tests are not reading tests.

11. When the results of your diagnostic tests show there are no serious deficiencies in a child's background, proceed with the work of the current year.

12. With bright children, who have mastered all of the previous material, you will be using your diagnostic tests as stepping stones to further achievement. They will be useful for selecting areas of interest for the child to pursue, for example.

13. In developing your diagnostic tests, stress concepts, not fact memorization.

14. At the beginning of the term, a diagnostic test will take several days to a week.

Divide it into a number of parts. While the children are taking the second part, you can be working with the first.

15. Develop a recording and filing system for yourself. You may prefer a notebook, with a page for each child. If you prefer, you can use a 5 x 7 file card. Divide it into subject areas. As you grade Part I of your diagnostic test, indicate:

Satisfactory, or needs work.
After reteaching a unit, indicate the result.

You may wish to record the material you use. If so, design a code so that you do not have to spend an inordinate amount of time in the bookkeeping. Use key numbers—so that when you need to know what was in Part I of your diagnostic test you can easily look it up.

Motivating the children

Our youngsters, from the day we meet them, are thinking, logical human beings. If we do not talk down to them, if they understand exactly what we are doing, if they feel their work in school is serious business, we can do a far better job of helping them to learn.

Make sure they understand your methods of teaching. Discuss with them the purpose of individualizing instruction. Show them specifically how it works, and how it will benefit them. No abstracts here, please. This is concrete, basic information. Give the child the satisfaction of realizing, "I can read the symbols on a weather map, now." The child who has had difficulty learning will truly benefit from this.

Explain that every child learns at a different rate, and that every one has some area he has not mastered.

The time you spend motivating your teaching, and giving the children an understanding of goals, and working to achieve them will be very well spent. Far too many children graduate from school with learning deficiencies which hamper them greatly. Show your children how this system attempts to eliminate this.

Informal diagnosis by examination of written work

1. First and foremost, every child should have a notebook. (Even first graders should be told to get one. They enjoy this since it gives them a sense of importance.)

2. Teach the children to use the notebook for note-taking and for recording their homework assignments. Have the actual assignments done on separate sheets of paper to be handed in and graded.

Children are often asked by parents, "What did you learn in

school today?" The notebook is concrete evidence that work is going on.

3. For older children, a looseleaf is essential. They will be working on contracts which should be kept together.

4. It will be wise for you to examine and correct the notebook periodically. Examine it carefully to determine what the child is doing incorrectly. Is he completing his work or not? Does it show indifference? Or lack of knowledge of the subject being taught?

5. Use the notebook to encourage creativity. Suggest the children use their notebooks to "do their own thing." The artist can illustrate it, the writer can put in short stories or poems, the little cook can put in recipes. Even doodlers should be encouraged to do designs. Many boys love to draw cars or planes. Have them feel they are doing constructive work by giving it a place in their notebooks. Perhaps, one day, one will become a car designer. Why not?

6. What if you discover children who are unable to write? Handwriting has become a lost skill, but is still a necessary one. Many children need training in penmanship—need it desperately. Some have never really been taught to write. No matter what subject you teach, isn't it your province to teach enough penmanship to make sure your children can write legibly enough to be understood?

How to make the results of your diagnostic tests work

1. Correcting diagnostic tests takes much time and effort. If you use short answer questions for at least half of each test, the grading is made simpler.

2. a. After you've graded the tests, study each. What areas of the child's knowledge are lacking? Compose a master list of exercises for teaching each of the areas you tested for. Then, using this list, work up a program for each child. State the goal clearly, so the child knows what skill he is working on—be it dividing by 9, or the use of "to," "too" and "two."

b. Some children will need more exercises than others, of course. There may even be a few with perfect results. For these have enrichment material available.

c. After a child has done the work, have him test himself, and correct his own paper; if he satisfactorily completes the unit, he may proceed to the next area of work.

   d. While the youngsters are working on the exercises, have a short conference with each to check his progress, and make sure he knows exactly what he is doing.

   e. If there were children with perfect or near perfect diagnostic tests, allow them to tutor some of the slower children in the class.

   f. Encourage the child who is having difficulty to seek help. Try to find the means to teach him a specific item—even if it requires several different approaches.

Grouping children with similar needs

In the test described above, you may find three or four children having difficulty with one type of problem. Experiment with methods for teaching it by presenting it to all of the children who need it at one time. By working with a group of children who have similar needs, you can save time and effort. Also, encourage the children to ask questions—for when one asks a question, quite often the others do not understand that point either.

Encourage the children to work together in such cases. They can actually help one another think situations and problems through.

Keep your groups flexible. Once the need for the group has ceased to exist, disband it. Thus, if you form a group to teach dividing by fractions, when the children have mastered it, disband the group.

Never let the youngsters get the idea they are in groups because they are slow in learning. A group exists only for a short time—to teach a particular problem or area. Keep your groups fluid and in motion. Once a child has mastered the material you have seen he requires, move him. Children are affected by stigmas. If it is even implied they are stupid, they become upset or hostile. It becomes even easier for them to shut you out—because they are hurt. We heard of one first grade class which had reading groups. One was the redbirds, another the bluebirds, another the yellowbirds and another the sparrows. One little boy complained to the teacher, "I don't want to be a sparrow. They're dumb birds. That's the dumb-dumbs." How painful for a child to have to think or admit this! And how unnecessary! If your groups are called the "sl group" or the "oi group," and they are changed frequently, hopefully the children will not think of themselves as slow.

Motivation: showing the child he can learn

There are children who are very motivated to learn, but for every one of these, there are four or five or seven or ten who are not. Our job is to motivate them—by every device, every method, every technique we can think of. We can use our individualization of instruction for motivation. By showing the child he can learn, he can be successful, he can achieve, he is motivated to try.

The old adage, "If at once you don't succeed, try, try again," is true. If you have to, you'll try again, but you won't want to. Failure is insidious. A young child tries to do cursive writing. He may not have sufficiently developed motor skills, and he fails. What happens to his enthusiasm? If you encounter this situation, change the material the child is working on. Find something he can do, (drawing and printing) and have him work at that. Then, gradually work him into the cursive writing.

On whatever grade level you teach, begin the year with a project each child can do successfully. Offer a number, and have the child select the one he prefers. For example, for young children, consider:

> Collecting different rocks.
> Collecting different leaves.
> Collecting picture postcards.
> Making a color wheel.
> Making a food chart.
> Making a dessert chart.
> Making an animal chart.
> Making a flower chart.
> Making a picture dictionary.
> Making a word wallet.
> Making a game chart.
> Making a story chart.

These projects can be handled by every child. Discuss the choice of topic with each child, and help him find one he really likes. Even baseball or football is acceptable.

In the higher grades, here are possibilities—listed merely to give you ideas.

> Famous people.
> Famous paintings.
> Current events.
> What's new in our town.
> Foods you should try.
> Books you should read.
> Sports you should try.
> Stamp collection.
> Coin collection.
> Ways of having fun.
> Places to visit.
> Experiments to do.

All projects should be done as charts or booklets—requiring pictures, (cut out of old books, magazines and the like) drawings, diagrams, or with real material pasted on them. But make sure every child has the materials, can do the job and, when it is completed, put it on display.

This is important. Let us explain why.

Far too many children are conditioned to fail. They start out in school, and never, but really never, accomplish anything of which they can be proud. It is almost as if they are failures from the first day. Yet, how can this be? If we are teaching them—on their level—as individuals how can they help but learn?

A little one loves nursery rhymes. Wonderful. Start on his chart or booklet, and help him. Just a simple booklet can delight him. Fold construction paper in half, and half again. Voila. The beginnings of the booklet. Now, cut out photos, or draw simple diagrams for him to trace or color. The artists among us might argue, "Allow the child to be free." If he wishes to draw, of course, but, if he prefers to trace, fine. The point is to produce a product of which *the child can be proud.*

Find a number of devices at which your children can be successful. Then, bit by bit, build on this. As we learned from Pavlovian experiments, we should condition our children—to succeed.

We know of the large number of children who have difficulty reading. Yet they learn to read brand names while very young children as they watch television. You might want to adopt this with retarded readers. Have word cards, and flash words at them. We have seen this done, eminently effectively, by a brand new teacher, who made the children feel they can succeed.

Teaching responsibility

If you can condition your children to enjoy completing work, you condition them to one of the very important aspects of learning. If you can teach them this is their responsibility, you accomplish even more. So many of our children do not feel they are responsible for their work. If they feel like doing the assignment, they do it. If they aren't in the mood, they don't bother. We, as teachers, must show them that each one is responsible. How? By discussing the problem with any and every child who shows a tendency to ignore this responsibility. By making the child aware of why the assignment is given, and how he should go about solving it. By stressing the positive—"I know you can do this work, Johnny. What do you think? Can you be responsible for it?" Unless we teach in this way, we are not preparing our youngsters for the world of school or of work later on.

Individualizing instruction is one of the educator's answers to today's problems. It is based on an understanding of the needs of the individual child. These needs are concrete—be they to learn to form a letter so it is legible, or to determine distance on a map. We recall one little boy who took map reading very seriously. "I'm going to be a policeman," he said, wide-eyed, "and you know how far they have to travel."

By diagnostic testing, we are able to learn of the children's topic deficiencies, so that, one by one, we can eliminate them. Using these tests can help you—so that, as far as your pupils are concerned, you are no longer the lady in the dark.

2

*Establishing goals and
planning lessons that
individualize instruction*

In the first chapter, you read about diagnosis and individualizing instruction in terms of skills and subject matter. In this chapter, we will discuss these aspects, plus the development of the child as a comfortable, functioning human being.

What are your children's needs? If you can determine these, you are able to individualize your instruction to really help the youngsters. You will be able to judge, when you have worked with them for even a short period of time, what some of their needs are. Others take longer to ferret out. Perhaps we can help you to pinpoint some of them, for your consideration.

1. Do your children need to learn to communicate? Is Nancy very quiet because she cannot express herself? Does John avoid talking because he doesn't know the appropriate words, and does he point, instead? Can your boys and girls reach one another with their thoughts and ideas? This is one of the basics of living in a society, and yet it is amazing how many people have difficulty in expressing themselves. Teaching children, all of the children, to communicate must be one of your prime goals—particularly those youngsters who show they are having some difficulty in getting their ideas across to others.

2. Do your children realize they are members of a group, and, as

such, must be able to function that way? In other words, they must be taught not to be self-centered. This comes as a shock to some youngsters, who have had little contact with other children. By stressing the group aspect of the class, and developing feelings of responsibility to one another, you help the children to become functioning members of their, and our, society.

3. Another goal you will want to establish for yourself is creating in each child a desire to learn. Call it curiosity, or motivation, if you like, but this thirst for learning can have a positive effect on the child's entire future. If it is never developed, the child may miss out on many of the important things in life.

4. The birthright of every child is the right to read—and this cannot be denied to any child. No matter which grade a youngster is in, or which subject he is being taught, it is necessary to teach him vocabulary and reading comprehension—for without these the child is virtually doomed, academically. The inability to read can be likened to intellectual blindness, placing impossible hurdles for the child to leap.

5. In individualizing instruction, you will develop one-to-one relationships with each child. This will give you the opportunities to recognize those children who have anti-social tendencies. You can work with the youngsters to bring this behavior out into the open, where it can be counteracted.

Helen, aged 6, grade 1, was a child who stole. Unfortunately, she was extremely talented in this area. She was an attractive little girl, with a soft voice, and gentle manners—and her teacher was very fond of her. In fact, she charmed most adults. It was hard to believe one's own eyes, when one actually saw her stealing another child's pencils, or crayons or money. When asked why she did these things, she said she didn't know. Once she said she liked crayons and pencils. Her teacher suggested she come to her desk whenever she wanted to use any of these things, and that the teacher would be happy to lend them to her. The teacher worked with the child for a few minutes daily, using a warm, friendly approach.

One day, to the surprise of everyone who knew Helen, the child entered the assistant principal's office, and emptied into the supervisor's lap a pencil case full of pencils and crayons.

"Here," she said, "I found these."

After that, Helen never took any other child's property. Of course she had been praised lavishly by her friend, the teacher, and by the assistant principal for having conquered this bad habit.

Credit Official Photograph, Bd. of Ed., N.Y.C.

Figure 2-1

You will encounter children with anti-social tendencies. As one of your goals, work with them. This requires much patience. Be constructive. Talk to the child. Show him why his behavior is anti-social. Give him good reasons for changing. Show him the hazards involved in the negative behavior. Try to develop a sense of conscience by showing, for example, how unfair it is to take someone else's property.

If you scream, chastise or severely punish a child, you may frighten the child temporarily—but only temporarily. On the other hand, if you can help to develop his conscience, you can permanently change his behavior, and so save him from performing anti-social acts which can mar his entire life—and even, possibly lead to dire consequences.

A child often steals because its an adventurous act. If you can provide healthful adventure, this desire will have a normal channel, rather than an anti-social one.

From the very first grade, teach your children good manners. For example, if a child accidentally pushes another, teach him to say "Excuse me. I didn't mean to push you." Teach the other child to respond, "That's O.K." or "That's alright." Teach the children some phrases that they can use to express themselves pleasantly rather than negatively. For instance, the simple "please" or "thank you," "pardon me" or "I'm sorry" are invaluable in the course of daily living. You can have skits or role playing showing these in action. Children often do not know how to respond to what may be, for them, an embarrassing situation.

In this one-to-one relationship, you can also discover serious personality problems or problems of other types. For instance—a vision or hearing defect, or a physical or intellectual infirmity can be spotted more easily when you are working with a single child. If you suspect a problem, refer the child to the guidance department, or to the nurse or doctor so that remedial measures may be taken. Many reading problems stem from visual defects. Some of these are not detected by the Snellen eye chart test, but require an examination by a competent physician. If you find a child can't read, don't accept this lying down. Do everything you can think of to ferret out the cause of his inability to read. You will find much information of value in subsequent chapters.

Personality defects may be even more serious. No matter what his age is, if a child appears troubled and if you see his notebook is filled with drawings of guns and knives, or soldiers at war, refer that child immediately to the guidance counselor, school psychologist or the principal. The chances are this child may be seriously disturbed emotionally, and if so, psychiatric treatment is a must. We believe that many murders, assassinations, and other serious crimes could have been prevented if timely psychiatric aid had been given when the perpetrator was a child. An ounce of prevention is worth not a pound, but a million pounds of cure.

Goals for every child

The goals you establish with each child will differ as his abilities and talents differ. No two children are alike, and no two learn at exactly the same rate. Furthermore, what is one child's meat is another child's poison. You will be changing goals constantly. The entire basis of individualized instruction is built on this forward movement of the child and of his goals.

How do you establish goals for every child?

Before you can begin individualizing your instruction, you must get to know your children. With the older ones, let us say even in the third grade—and above—we suggest you begin by having the youngsters write an autobiography. While they are writing it, you can speak to each one, individually. By adroit questioning, you can learn much about him.

First, motivate the writing of the autobiography. Do this by reading aloud excerpts from the autobiography of a famous person—BUT ONE WITH WHOM THE CHILDREN WILL RELATE. On the first day of class, or subsequently, ask the children "whose autobiography or biography would interest you?" If they don't know what an autobiography or a biography is, define it. Then have a class discussion to determine whose life shall be looked into. Your class might even decide on two—a man and a woman. Then, the next day read portions aloud to them. Try to select the most interesting incidents. Next, work out with the children a series of questions they can answer in their own autobiographies. Assure the children anything they have to say will be held in the strictest confidence.

Ask the children to write this as a paragraph, rather than merely answering the questions. This will give you a sampling of their ability to write, and their skill level to date.

Here are some questions you might wish to include:

1. Whom do you live with? (Not "Write about your family" because many children are in foster homes.)
2. Where and when were you born?
3. If you are a boy, do you like being a boy—and why? If you're a girl, do you like being a girl and why?
4. Do you have brothers and sisters? Which? How old are they?
5. Are you happy at home? Why?
6. Are you happy in school? Why?
7. Are there some things you would like to change in your family life, or your school life? Why?
8. Are you in good health? If not, what is your problem?

9. What is your favorite subject?
10. Which subjects do you dislike and why?
11. Do you have difficulty doing your homework?
12. Which sports, if any, do you like?
13. Which foods do you like and which do you dislike?
14. Do you like most people? Why or why not?
15. How many hours of television do you watch a week?
16. Which are your favorite programs?
17. What's your favorite color?
18. What would you do if you wanted to really have a good time?

Remind the children to write their answers in the form of a composition (especially if they are in fourth grade or above). This will enable you to see their written language skills, as well as learn about their personalities.

While the children are working on this autobiography, you will have an opportunity to walk around the room working with them individually.

Whenever you assign work of this nature, some children will finish more quickly than others. When a child is ready to submit his work, have him bring it to you. Review it rapidly. If it appears well done, accept it. If it is shoddy, return it, to be redone. Don't ever say "This is poor work," though. On the contrary, make the child feel that he can do better. Find something in the composition which is good—a word or a sentence—and point this out to him. Show him why its good, and encourage him. Don't ever take a defeatist attitude toward any child. If the child needs help work with him yourself, or assign one of the more skilled children to work with him (after the latter has completed his own assignment).

The autobiography is a major piece of work. It should take time. Stress this with the children.

Do not accept shoddy work. Only if children are instructed to do quality work will they ever learn to do it. If you impress this upon them, you can get them to produce fine work. We live in an era in which we are seeing much shoddiness in manufacturing, as well as in thinking. It's up to us, in our limited sphere, to improve it.

When a child has handed in a satisfactory paper, permit him to select a book or magazine and read, or look at the pictures. You will need a selection. You may be able to borrow these from the school library, or from other teachers. Children may be encouraged to bring in their own books or magazines. Always "borrow" these—and return them at the end of the term—or when they have outlived their usefulness. Sports magazines are important—even if it means subscribing to one or two to obtain them. Even some comic books are worthwhile. Screen them carefully and obtain permission from your supervisor for their use in class.

Have library monitors whose responsibility it is to keep the library in perfect order.

This library will serve many purposes. The most important is that it will encourage the children to want to read.

A word about satisfactory work. If Mary is capable of much better work than John, her level of "satisfactory" is higher than John's. But do not make John's so low that it cheats him. Be sure he is learning to do good work, too. Never make odious comparisons.

Avoid derogatory statements about any child. Show him how he can improve himself.

Using the conventional lesson plan

Both skills and subject matter can be taught effectively by using the more-or-less conventional lesson plan. As you probably know, this plan consists of six important parts—the aim of the lesson (for every lesson must have an aim), the motivation, the concepts taught, the pivotal questions, the materials needed, and the individualization of the lesson.

Let us, for example, take the well loved poem, "The Children's Hour" written by Henry Wadsworth Longfellow.

First, let us consider the *aim* in teaching this poem. It might well be a two-fold-first, an enjoyment of poetry by familiarizing the children with these delightful verses, and second, to teach the children *to love*. (A famous writer was once asked what words he wanted inscribed on his tombstone. His answer was "Say, that I loved.")

Second, how can we *motivate* this lesson? Very simply, by suggesting that this poem be used as a nucleus for entertainment provided for an assembly period.

Third, what *concepts* do you wish to impress upon the children—have the children read aloud the parts of the poem they find most significant? Do they find a message in these verses? Let us ask the children how the ideas in this poem can be used to make their own lives richer and happier. Could a "Children's Hour" be created in their own home? Would it benefit them? How might it help a family to become happier?

Fourth, by skillful *questioning* (rather than lecturing) elicit the moral worth, as well as the tenderness of feeling in these verses. Let the children find the parts of this poem that express these sentiments and read them aloud.

Fifth, by having the necessary *materials* on hand, the actual teaching of the lesson is facilitated. In this instance, every child should be furnished with a copy of "The Children's Hour."

Lastly, let us *individualize* the lesson by assigning work to each child. This may be done by groups or individually. The homework assignment might grow out of this. Let us consider what assignments might be the outgrowths:

An appreciative reading or recitation of the poem.

The writing of verses and essays relevant to the poem.

Making drawings or paintings, illustrating the scenes found in the poem.

Converting "The Children's Hour" into a playlet or a musical.

Unit plans make individualization easier

If your work is planned in terms of units, you will find it much simpler to individualize work for your children.

What is a unit? Usually it is a major topic and, as such, appears in your curriculum. It must be finite, however. One cannot expect children to learn all about the United States in six weeks.

If your curriculum is not divided into units, use your textbook to help you. Generally, you can link chapters into meaningful segments of work.

A unit will contain approximately six to twenty lessons. Because it is a broader division, you can select the areas on which you wish to concentrate with each child. Linked to each unit should be skill development, and it is here that the individualizing is most important.

If you wish, you may work out a number of assignments for a

unit, ranging from ones suitable for the slowest child to work for the most advanced. Perhaps there will be five or six. Perhaps eight. But then, suit the assignment to the child's ability. Make each a bit more than the child can handle comfortably. Most often assignments are merely rehashing of material taught in class. They stimulate few of the youngsters, if any. Make yours stimulating. How? Call on your own resources. What interests you? What have you learned that interests your children? Work from these interests outward.

Lisa is interested in poetry. You're teaching a unit on weather. How far apart are science and poetry? Never too far. Ask Lisa to study clouds, and learn the different types—cumulus, alto-cumulus, etc., with their characteristics. Then allow her to find examples of how various poets, both contemporary and traditional, described them. Jonie Mitchell's lovely song "Both Sides Now" is often called "Clouds." It describes them as "feather canyons," for instance.

Another child is more purely scientifically inclined. Perhaps he can investigate the formation of clouds. Still another might build a cloud chamber.

But what about the child who isn't interested in anything that is linked to your subject? Talk to him. Offer a list of suggestions, and permit him to choose one.

These are long assignments, requiring thought and effort. They do not preclude short reviews of subject matter. They are the individualized aspect of the unit.

Using a planbook or index cards

You may find index cards to be a big improvement over a planbook, or you may find a combination of both suits you best. For individualized assignments, we have found the index cards are excellent. They may be distributed to the children, collected after they are used, kept filed (by a card monitor) in a shoebox.

For the unit plan, with the component daily lessons, we found a looseleaf book was the most efficient format.

Your planning will be very personalized and suited to you and your children.

For every unit you teach, work out a series of objectives. These should be finite learnings you expect the children to master. They must be limited in scope, and within the range of the children's comprehension. They should be such that every child should be able to master each one. In other words, if there are ten objectives, you and the children should work to reach all ten. They should be exciting enough to hold the children's interest.

A sample unit for the second grade

As an example, let us take the following story as a unit for the second grade—with the objectives you might use in teaching it. The basic purpose is to teach reading and phonics. However, spelling, vocabulary building, social studies and drawing are also desirable areas stemming from this unit.

Here is the story: Print it and rexograph or use a large chart.

PUSSYCAT AND LITTLE BROWN BIRD

Once upon a time, there was a pretty white pussy cat. Her name was Kitty. Kitty lived with her Mommy Pussy cat in the country. One day, while she was sitting under a tree, Kitty looked up and saw a little brown bird. He was a very happy little bird. He was singing and singing. Kitty said to the little brown bird "I am going to catch you and eat you up!"

"Why do you want to eat me up?" said the little brown bird.

"Because I am hungry," said Kitty.

"Go home to your Mommy. She will give you some milk."

"No, no, no," said naughty little Kitty. "I don't want any milk. I want you!"

"Well," said the little brown bird. "You can't have me! You can't have me!"

"Why not?" said the naughty little pussy cat.

"Because you cannot fly and I can fly! Now, see me fly!" and the little brown bird flew away up high. Then, he flew higher and higher and higher; and he said "You naughty little pussy cat, you can't catch me, you can't catch me!"

Kitty jumped up high into the tree, but she could not catch the little brown bird. So she began to cry, "Meow, meow, meow, meow!" But the little brown bird flew far, far, away.

Kitty ran home to her Mommy crying "Meow, meow, meow."

"Why are you crying, Kitty?" said her Mommy.

"I am crying because I could not catch a little brown bird."

"Why did you want to catch a poor little brown bird?" said the Mommy Pussy cat.

"I wanted to catch the little brown bird because I wanted to eat her up."

"If you were a little brown bird, would you like someone to eat you up?" asked the Mommy Pussy cat.

"No, no, no," said Kitty. "I would not like that at all! But I am hungry Mommy. I am very, very hungry!"

"Well, if you promise me, that you will never try to catch the little brown bird again, I will give you some milk."

"I promise, I promise, I promise!" said Kitty. "So, please, Mommy, give me some milk."

So, the kind Mommy Pussy cat gave Kitty some milk. She drank it all up. And Kitty and her Mommy and the little brown bird lived happily forever after.

These are the objectives:

1. The child must show he understands the story by answering these questions:

   a. Who are the animals in the story?
   b. What did Kitty wants to do?
   c. Why did she want to do this?
   d. Why couldn't she do what she wanted to do?
   e. Why did she cry, "Meow, meow, meow?"
   f. How did the mommy pussy cat help her child?
   g. Why did they all live happily ever after?

2. The child must recognize the salient words:

pussy cat	she	cannot
kitty	catch	fly
mommy	milk	high
little	no	higher
brown	naughty	jumped
bird	because	tree
meow	promise	lived
far	some	happily
crying	please	forever
hungry	kind	after
very	drank	

3. The ability to master the phonic elements of these words.

cat: bat, fat, hat, mat, Nat, pat, rat, sat, vat.
she: be, he, me, we, the.
no: go, so.
fly: why, shy, try, by, my, sty, cry.
not: hot, pot, rot, jot, cot, lot, tot.
ran: ban, Dan, can, fan, man, Nan, pan, van.
up: cup, pup.

4. The ability to spell the simple salient words.

cat
she
fly

5. The ability to spell words having the same phonetic element.

All words belonging to the phonic family as cat.
All words belonging to the phonic family as she.
All words belonging to the phonic family as fly.

6. The ability to recognize words within the salient words.

pussy   high (in higher)
cat   want (in wanted)
                           cry (in crying)
                           forever

7. The ability to build words using the phonetic elements outlined in item #3.

8. The ability to understand the structure of a simple declarative sentence.

Pick out three declarative sentences.
Give the first word of three sentences.
Give the last word of three sentences.

9. The ability to write a simple declarative sentence. Have the child write four such sentences.

10. The use of the capital letter in introducing the simple declarative sentence.

11. The use of the period at the end of the sentence.

12. In social studies, can the child see how this story applies to the adage, "Do unto others as you would have others do unto you"?

13. Have the child master the meanings of the new words in the story and words that are developed in the phonic section.

vat	jot	van
shy	tot	country
sty	ban	naughty

Using the story to the fullest extent

This will depend on your class; upon its previous learning, and on its intelligence. Every child of normal intelligence should be able to master these objectives with relatively little difficulty. There will be some, however, who will require individualized instruction. The one-to-one relationship will facilitate the mastery of these objectives.

To teach the word recognition, you may have the children make flash cards from drawing paper or oaktag. (They should be visible in any part of the classroom.) Many games can be devised using these flash cards. Have every child make three of a different word. You supply the model, working at the board. Collect the flash cards. The children have now made the materials for the game.

Hold up one flash card at a time. Each child gets a chance to read it. If he reads the word correctly, he gets the card. When all the cards have been used, the child who has the most cards wins the game, and is awarded some small prize.

The ingenious teacher may devise many games with words. Thus a love of words is fostered, and reading becomes fun for the children.

To teach sentence structure, we used the following to catch and hold the children's attention.

The teacher asks, "How many children have a dog at home?"

"If your dog is hungry, does he say I'm hungry?" (The youngsters love this. They laugh.) "What does he say?"

"How many children have a cat at home? If the cat is hungry, what does she say?"

"Who has a baby at home? What does the baby do if he's hungry? The baby begins to cry."

"Do you cry when you want something? No, you don't cry. You ask for it. What do you say if you want some candy? You say 'I want some candy.' "

"What did you use? You used words, didn't you?"

"And so, when you think of something you want to say, you use the words. Now tell me something you want to say."

The children will construct sentences for you—probably very much alike in content, but sentences, nevertheless, such as "I like candy." or "I want a kitten."

Then say, "When we have thought of something we want to say, and we say it, we have a sentence."

(One little one said, as we were developing this lesson, "It's like a little tiny story.")

Now the children are ready to write a sentence. They examine the sentences in their books, and the teacher asks, "How do we begin every sentence in the whole world?" The children will tell you they begin with a capital letter.

Then ask, "What do you find at the end of each sentence?" Some bright child will say, "Most of the time it's a period."

The teacher writes on the board, the children in their notebooks. The teacher writes slowly, word by word. The children say the words as they write them, again emphasizing the capital and the period.

After this, the teacher checks their notebooks. The children who have mastered writing the sentence can go on to making picture dictionaries, or other creative work, while the teacher gives individualized instruction to the children who have not yet mastered it.

The contract

One of the devices being used today to individualize instruction is the contract. It usually covers a unit of work, and is varied to suit the needs and abilities of the individual child.

He or she is given a comprehensive assignment, consisting of a number of pages of work to be completed. Various resources are suggested including textbooks, library books, film strips, records, films and transparencies. The child learns to use these materials in his problem solving. (See Chapter 10.)

Taking into consideration the differing rates of learning

The rate at which individuals learn differs from person to person, and also from subject to subject. Have you ever taught a topic, and observed how much more quickly some children grasp the material than others. This is evident most often in arithmetic, where sometimes the brightest will require only one explanation for a procedure, while others will require many discussions and lessons before they "get it." Then, too, the same child who is a whiz at math may take much longer to learn to hit a baseball. Yet hitting the ball is a form of learning, as well.

You probably learn relatively quickly. Most teachers do. Have you ever found yourself in an area where you had a hard time learning? It is an experience we feel every teacher should have. One of the authors encountered it trying to learn to play tennis. The frustration was very real—and it gave her a greater understanding of how a child must feel who is having difficulty learning to read.

In your class, you probably have some children who learn after you have taught them something once. One review for reinforcement is generally enough. What happens by the third time you present the material? Of course, they get bored. This is one reason to individualize your instruction:

1. Assign different work to the children who have learned the topic you are teaching.

2. Try having them teach some of the others.

3. Allow them time for individualized reading. There is no reason children cannot read while they are in school, "On school time."

Using a variety of approaches

When you teach a topic, and the children don't learn it, do you teach it exactly the same way a second time? If your results have been good with most of the class, then, of course, you'll stay with this procedure. However, if you find your results are not as satisfactory as you would like them to be, try changing your approach to the subject.

First; check to make sure the youngster understands the words you are using. One teacher used the word "different" very often with her second graders. One day, she overheard a youngster say to another, "What's different?" The teacher thought the child asked the question in reference to the subject, but then she heard him say, "What is this 'different' she says all the time?"

Second; check to see if the area you are teaching is dependent on any previous teaching, and if the child has the background he needs. If he doesn't, of course he will have trouble.

Third; question the child. Break down the topic into a series of questions. Try to determine at just which point the youngster doesn't understand! Teach from there.

Fourth; ask a bright child to teach the topic. You may find his approach different—and helpful.

Fifth; discuss the matter with your colleagues. Often they can give you ideas.

Keeping your planning flexible

If you can keep your planning flexible, you will find your work far simpler than if you try to work in a very rigid framework.

Of course you must plan—if you don't, neither you nor the children will know what is going on. Discuss your plans with the class. At the start of each unit, determine, together, what the objectives are, and how they can best be achieved. Determine which activities will be involved, but be prepared to change them if better ones are suggested.

Class 8BX was doing a unit on geology. As they discussed the various types of rocks which make up the earth's crust, one child said, "There's an old quarry way back of the church in Graniteville. We could visit it." They could, and did. They discovered that the community had been named Graniteville erroneously, because it was built on basalt, rather than on granite. Several trips to gather rocks came out of that first expedition, and the children were thrilled to find serpentine, as well, in a nearby area.

One teacher, struggling to help each child learn arithmetic, found that the youngsters loved the idea of a store. One was "built" at the back of the room, and the children progressed much more rapidly when the work was related to buying and selling merchandise.

Using your plans as a record for future reference

One thinks he will remember everything covered in class, but it doesn't work that way. Why not keep a record? Especially since you have already done a good deal of the work on it. You've written your plan. Make use of it for this purpose.

As you write your plans, leave space to add to them. Then, after you've used the plans, write your notes right on them. Indicate changes which came about as you taught the unit. The additions you made are important. So are the subtractions—because its a good idea to indicate where the lesson fell down—if it did. Which areas did not interest the children, for example, and where were emergency repairs necessary.

When you have to reteach part of the unit, indicate how you did this. Put into all of your written plans the individualization you did. Then, when you teach the unit again, much of the thinking you did will come back to you, if you use your plans as a reminder.

Even if you are teaching another unit, you can read over your plans for ideas. Many methods are useful for other topics as well. We have found ideas to be extremely elusive. By writing them down, they are yours to keep.

Summary

In this chapter we have discussed establishing goals for the teacher for each child. In addition to skills and subject matter, the teacher's goals should include teaching every child to communicate, making him aware that he is a member of a group, and must function with the others, developing a desire to learn in each youngster, teaching him to read, and working with those pupils who have anti-social tendencies.

We suggest you get to know your children by having them work on an autobiography.

The conventional lesson plan and the unit plan are discussed, with a sample unit given, that may be used with the second grade.

It is essential that, in your planning, you take into consideration the differing rates of learning which are present among the youngsters in your class. For those children who are slow, a variety of approaches to a topic is preferable to repeating what you have already taught—in the same way in which you have taught it. By keeping your plans flexible, you are able to make your work easier, and the class far more interesting. Your plans form a valuable record of your work to which you can always refer.

3

Measuring the basic psychological needs of each child

The basic psychological needs of every child

The basic psychological needs of every child are to be needed, to be wanted, to be loved, and to have a personal image of self-worth. The bulk of the responsibility for fulfilling these needs lies with the parents. They deal with the child from the cradle—really from the day he is born. If we accept modern views of psychological development, we realize that their influence is tremendous, indeed. However, as teachers, we, too, have a great effect on the child's development. Our real sphere of influence is in the area of helping the child to see himself as a worthwhile person—to develop his feelings of self-esteem and importance.

Why every child needs to build a positive self-image and how individualized instruction can foster this

Have you, as an adult, ever in your lifetime had the experience of failure? Have you tried to accomplish something and not been able to do it? If not, you owe it to your development as a teacher to place yourself, somehow, in this situation. Why? Because, most often teachers do not realize what it means to be unsuccessful. Most teachers go through school with relative ease. They have no idea what it means to fail—again and again. Yet this is what some of our children are up against. Be it reading, or arithmetic, there are those who just can't understand and learn it. Their sense of failure is almost obvious—if you are tuned in to it. If your individualized instruction program is to succeed, you must have some measure of each child's self-image, and his feelings of self-worth.

How can you get this?

Study your children by observation of their appearances and their work. Be perceptive. As Hamlet says, there are those who "seeing all, see nothing." Does the child appear to be trying, or has he ceased to do so? So often the child who sees himself as a failure has stopped making the effort.

We can begin to build the self-image of each child by having every one contribute to the classroom environment in some specialty or area. For instance, exhibit the work of every child who can draw, paint, or write. What if a child is poor in these areas? If he has any organizational ability, allow him to take charge of the class library, of the textbooks, of the supplies, of the closets.

> Care of plants
> Care of fish
> Cutting out and mounting pictures
> Photographer
> Milk monitor

Another way to build up a child's self-image is through assembly programs. Here you can use the talents of the writer, the actor, the stage manager, the business manager, the musician, the dancer. There are other ways to make children feel they excel. Athletics and singing can also accomplish this. Perhaps you can allow certain children to teach.

In all of these ways the development of self-worth is fostered.

Conversely, if a child is discouraged, the ill effects can be very far reaching. The teacher can have a devastating influence upon a child's personality.

Joshua, who is quite a scholar of world affairs, starts to stutter whenever he begins to discuss them. As a youngster in the fifth grade, he remembers having been asked by his teacher to do a report. He was told to do a report on the republic and instead did it on the Republican party. When he brought in the report he was given a zero.

"Joshua, this was a stupid report. You should have known better. If you weren't sure, you should have consulted me. I'm surprised to find you so stupid." As a result of this incident, this child who is now an adult, still stutters whenever he begins a conversation concerning world affairs.

Have you ever told a child "You're stupid"? Even in jest, its deadly. The child may believe you—the idea may take root—and the youngster's self-esteem may be seriously damaged.

Jackie's parents called the junior high school he attended. They were frantic. Jackie had run away from home. When he was finally found, and questioned, he stated, "I was always called dumb-dumb. My brothers think its very funny. Maybe they're smarter than I am—but that doesn't make me a dumb-dumb."

We have mentioned in the previous chapter the establishment of individual goals. A child's self-esteem will be built up as he achieves these goals. If you assign tasks to him which are a challenge, but which he can accomplish, he gets to feel capable of handling his work.

There are children in our junior highs whose reading scores on standardized tests are 3.0. This would seem to indicate the child is reading on a third grade level. Actually, he is given this score for writing his name on the paper. Can you imagine how defeated he feels? The only possible solution to his severe reading problem is individualized instruction.

Giving every child responsibilities

If handled deftly, most children will welcome responsibilities. For example, meet Martin. Martin was often absent from school. He would stay home on the slightest provocation. One sneeze, and the child felt he had a severe cold. His mother went along with this behavior. Martin was definitely overprotected.

His astute teacher, however, looked for some responsibility she could give this child which would interest him. She noticed he often stared at the beautiful tropical fish tank displayed in the classroom.

One day, she asked Martin if he thought he could feed the fish. Martin jumped at the chance.

"But, Martin," the teacher said, "The fish are depending on you to be fed. You'll be keeping them alive."

Martin assured her that he could, indeed.

Several weeks later Martin appeared in school with a severe cold. "I told my mother I couldn't be absent, or my fish would die," he told his teacher. "In fact," he added with deep self-pride, "My mother wanted me to stay home—but I was afraid my fish would starve."

Classroom duties of this type can build the children's self-esteem. In his own eyes Martin became important.

In like manner, the responsibilities of learning should be presented to the children.

The goals of individualized instruction help the child to be aware of, and to assume, his learning responsibilities. This can have a profound effect on his intellectual development and on his wish to learn. When you show a child exactly what it is you expect of him, you give him a target to shoot at.

The well-known Coleman report brought out this concept. It is far more interesting if you experiment with it yourself. Actually tell your children you know they are going to do particularly well because of the new individualized instruction program that you are planning. Explain that every goal will be one that each child is capable of reaching.

Have the children graph their progress as a measure of their success. In this way, they can see their accomplishments. You can do this even in the lower grades, with simple graphs. As the children get older, use more complex means of diagramming their progress.

Remember, of course, that not all children will have the same objectives. Make sure the goals you assign to each child will be within his reach, particularly if he has shown academic deficiencies. He must, however, be challenged, for if the work is too simple, the child will not benefit from it, and will become bored.

The need for a physically beautiful environment, created and maintained by the children

"The apparel doth oft proclaim the man," said Polonius, in *Hamlet*. In like manner, the apparel worn by the classroom, doth oft proclaim the teacher and the class, for the classroom is veritably a second home. To even a casual observer, if the floor of a room is filled with papers, if the desks are strewn about, if there are no decorations, no evidence of the children's or teacher's interest, then one can sense the disinterestedness of both the children and the teacher. When substantial teaching and learning are going on, the room sings. Both teacher and children are proud of it.

Individualized instruction supplies the opportunities which enable each child to contribute to the vital appearance of the room.

A newspaper reporter asked to be permitted to visit the classrooms of an elementary school to find a possible human interest story. He entered one fifth grade classroom, and found his story. The entire back wall was filled with children's books, which had been written, illustrated, bound and displayed by the fifth graders. These included autobiographies, sports stories, and many science fiction and mysteries. Each child in the class had contributed in some measure. Some had written the stories, others illustrated them, and still others bound them. Vividly colored mounting paper had been used to make the setting more attractive.

The reporter was so impressed by the books, that he suggested a contest be held to select a winner. The prize set was the publication of the winning book. Can you imagine the excitement and the pleasure that this work engendered.

A beautiful classroom will bring out the best in the children as well as bringing pleasure to the teacher. It should be an expression of every child's effort.

Developing self-pride—"We write our own price tags"

Although derogatory remarks are damaging to the child's personality, encouraging words will do much to build a feeling of belonging and self-worth. We write our own price tags. Help the child to see himself as being worthy. *Find* something to like about every child—don't be afraid to express it. Surely we have all met children who are not likable. They are almost always the ones who need individualized instruction in social behavior the most.

To a child who laughs a lot in class, and might be inclined to be derisive, the teacher might say, "Jack, I'm glad you laugh so often. Come on—share the joke with us. Let us all enjoy it—and laugh with you."

To the child who tends to be a bully, try to channel his energies so that he becomes a help, rather than a hindrance, in the class. Work with him; try to get him to understand that his energies can be used constructively rather than destructively. By working with him individually, you can get through to him.

A young boy was once arrested for stealing. When he was brought before the court, the judge—a fine person—observed, while the boy was defending himself, that he had definite dramatic power. Instead of sending the boy to jail, the judge sent him to dramatic school. Some years later the boy became a well-known screen star. It was the judge's insight into the child's abilities, and his keen perception of the boy's artistic powers that enabled the youngster to become a well-loved member of society, instead of the inmate of a jail. In this case, the judge helped to write the price tag. His belief in the child made the child believe in himself.

Caring for living things

Children often feel insecure. They are, after all, small in size. In "olden times" they were considered to be miniature adults. Haven't you seen photographs of them—dressed exactly like little men and women? Today, we no longer think of them this way. However, we do know that the events which happen to youngsters can affect their entire lives. The child is, indeed, "father to the man."

Because of his small size, a child may feel inferior to adults—but inferior in terms of being almost helpless. Have you ever seen a little one cringe when an angry adult shouted at him? Children hate being screamed at. They also may interpret remarks literally.

We saw one little girl shriek in horror when told by her huge grandmother, "You're so adorable I could eat you up."

By giving children small, living things to care for, we show them, in a concrete manner, that they are powerful—that they are strong human beings. Peter, a seven-year-old, was very shy. He rarely spoke, preferring to hide his face with his hands. When he did speak, he whispered. One Monday morning, his teacher brought in a turtle. Peter's face lit up when he saw it. The teacher placed it on his desk, and Peter watched it.

"Tell us about the turtle, Peter," the teacher said. "You watch it and feed it, and then report back to the other children on Friday."

Peter took this assignment very seriously. He studied the turtle carefully and on Friday, he told the class; "The turtle is my friend. He knows me. When I come near the bowl he crawls over to see me." The teacher wondered about this fact, but not about Peter's reaction. It was obvious. He needed this pet, and he thrived on the responsibility of caring for it.

Children react in like manner to fish, chameleons, and even grasshoppers. It is essential to teach them, though, that small animals have short life spans, and that, if they die, it is not the child's fault. Raising goldfish or guppies, or any variety of tropical fish can be an excellent hobby—even for first graders. They can develop feelings of responsibility—and a love of nature and living things.

Children can be encouraged to talk about their younger brothers and sisters, for the same reasons—to show how they assume some responsibility for them. It makes our children feel "big"—and this feeling is good for them.

Developing feelings of accomplishment

Your entire individualized instruction program must be based on a positive approach to learning.

As soon as you teach a unit of any type to your children, give out worksheets. Have the class do the work, while you walk around, helping those boys and girls who require your assistance. When a child has successfully completed the work, allow him to select an activity from the list you have posted. (These will be discussed later.) Until a child has successfully completed the assignment, have him stay with it. In this way, he has to complete it before he moves on. Indicate his success by a mark on the worksheet.

Post the activities to be done after the regular work; these might differ from week to week.

For instance—reading library books; making puppets; working with wool or wire, making a scrap book that matches the child's personality and his talents. The youngster interested in athletics can make one on his favorite sport. The class poet can do a scrapbook on poems he writes or collects, in or out of school. The little cook can collect recipes.

It is important for the skills you are teaching to be learned first before the child goes on to these activities. The latter can be used to motivate him.

Children can benefit by tutoring one another. The slower child learns the material, and the brighter youngster learns to teach it. By teaching it, incidentally, the child will master the subject far more thoroughly.

Do not allow any child to neglect to finish his work. Every boy or girl needs to learn to complete tasks set for him. Learning this self-discipline can be an asset all of his life.

If the child's interest or ideas wane, the teacher or other children can remotivate him. This type of activity develops an *esprit de corps* amongst the students. They learn to learn and help learn.

Rewards for accomplishment

Every person, big or little, young or old, enjoys being rewarded for a job well done. Our pupils are no exception. We can use rewards for motivation. Indeed, they are among the best possible motivational devices.

Display an Honor Roll in your classroom. However, have a novel twist. Your Honor Roll is for Improvement, and should so state: "Honor Roll for Improvement in Work and Conduct."

If a child goes from 50 to 60 he is entitled to a place on this Honor Roll.

Of course, a child doing high grade work deserves a place on either this or another Honor Roll.

Attendance should be noted, and commended by placing the child's name on an attendance Honor Roll.

Make these Honor Rolls very attractive. Use colorful lettering and charts. Perhaps you can have your children, or upper grade youngsters, who are talented, make these charts.

Any progress should be noted on the Improvement Honor Roll. This includes behavior, academic learning, punctuality, or class citizenship.

You may wish to have the children make other charts for display; i.e., Class Helpers, Members of the Public Library, Always on Time.

Grades, too, are a form of reward. Be sure you mark fairly—and even generously. We have seen children fight for a point. This is wholesome. But they'll work much harder if you are fair, while generous, than if you are the "hard marker" who prides himself on being tough.

Rewards

Parties are an excellent form of reward. They add gaiety and enjoyment, as well as appreciation. And use your children to help. Every child can do something. Through the one-to-one relationship you'll find the youngster's talents. Use them! The artists decorate, the cooks prepare refreshments, the math student figures costs, and some of the children whose manners you want to improve, can act as hosts or hostesses.

Occasions for a party

Individualize parties—for instance, if a child returns after an illness, make a party. If a child does something noteworthy, make a party. A memorable example of this was the time a youngster saved two families from fire by awakening them. Her classmates made her a beautiful party to commemorate her heroism. You can even make a party if a child's behavior improves radically. If non-readers improve and, in the course of the term learn to read, make them a surprise party. Commendations and applause, given by the children as well as the teacher, will help develop an *esprit de corps.*

If you announce on Friday that there will be a party on Monday, this will bring the youngsters in on Monday. (Monday is often a poor day, attendance wise.)

A party need not be a very elaborate affair. Candy, milk and cookies, or ice cream—plus some games or stories, and favorite songs can do the trick.

During the party, give those commendations and applause to the child or children for whom the party was made. Use the "Surprise" approach. If you announce a party for Monday, don't tell for whom it is intended. In the course of the year, be sure every child is so honored, just as every boy or girl's name should appear on some Honor Roll.

If a class misbehaves, the party may be withheld. This is an excellent form of disciplining. Because the children want a party, they'll behave—and develop a sense of responsibility.

Of course you must know how to control the party. At a signal from you, the class must get quiet. Once trained this way, the children will enjoy parties—and so will you. This helps make your classroom a fun place.

On the junior high level, the youngsters might enjoy a 20-minute period Friday afternoon for playing records. We've seen this really motivate many classes.

Trips

Trips are another excellent educational tool that can be used as motivation and as a reward. A school trip is a way of escaping from the routine of the classroom, to the fascinating world outside. At least, that is how many children see it. We have capitalized on this by using the same trip as a reward.

Two English teachers decided to tell their classes they could take only half of each class on a trip. Pupils would be selected on the basis of who made the greatest effort. They found everyone trying—so much so, that they changed the set-up—and told the class anyone who tried his best would be invited. The children were actually disappointed. One teacher was told "You shouldn't change the rules in the middle of the game." The youngsters actually wanted the rewards to be real rewards.

Individualized trips

Some of your children are interested or drawn to music, others to art, still others to science. How can you manage to take them to the places from which they would profit the most? Actually there's a simple solution to this problem. Get together with two or three other teachers and work out your plans. Each takes a group to one type of place for which that group of children has shown a particular leaning. Take the musically-inclined children to a concert, the children with a scientific turn of mind to a museum of natural history, an aquarium, or even an airport, and the children with a leaning toward art to art galleries or an art museum.

Individualized commendation cards

Make commendation cards from varying-colored construction paper. You might have this done by the art department or the class artist. Thus, the incentive may reach the art department as well as the class artists.

Display the cards after they have been awarded by hanging them up in the classroom. At report card time, give the child his commendation card to take home. The purpose of the cards, then, is many fold. They are encouragement, they are attractive, and they please not only the child, but the parent, too. They forge a friendly link between the child, the teacher and the home.

Commendation letters

You may have your young children write in their best penmanship, letters to their parents in which they say:

"Dear Mother and Dad,

I am very happy to tell you that my teacher is very pleased with me."

_____

Child signs his name.

Then you, the teacher, add a sentence or two, such as:

"I enjoy having Billy in my class. He is very cooperative."

_____

Your signature.

This device, used only when the child deserves it, is another link between the home and the school. One parent showed such a letter to a teacher. It had been written by this teacher and her little pupil twenty-one years before.

Defeating the defeatist attitude

Praise, encourage, and smile at the child's efforts. Put your hand on his shoulder. Hug him. No child—and indeed no adult, does not respond to this type of behavior, but it is particularly important with children.

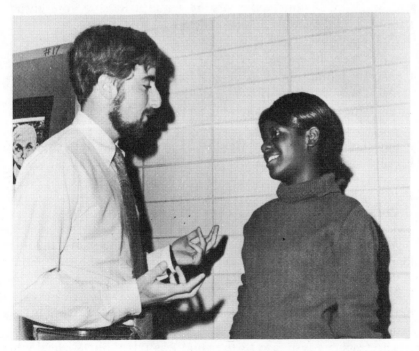

Credit Official Photograph, Bd. of Ed., N.Y.C.

Figure 3-1

One fine teacher was heard to respond to a child who said to her, "No one likes me!" "That isn't true."

Indeed, the teacher thought, as she looked at the child, "She's right, poor thing. No one gives a damn about her." But the teacher did. She said to the child, *"I* like you. *I* like you very much. Shall we be special friends?" This youngster happened to be an unattractive child. No visible effort by her parents had ever been made to make the child even presentable. Gently and deftly, the teacher talked with the child. She taught her, in detail, about keeping her clothes and person clean, and about her personal grooming. They even discussed the use of the voice, and physical and dental care. The child was sent to the dentist because her front teeth were actually rotting away. Most important of all, the teacher taught this little girl to smile. All this was possible because of the one-to-one relationship. This was truly individualized instruction—in living.

Throughout this book, you will find ways and means to help children. But they must be aware that you are helping them. They will be aware if your endeavors are genuine. Be sure your entire slant is upward. Never run a child down.

Can you picture a fine teacher ever telling a child that he is a cripple? Yet she would be doing just as grave an injustice by tauntingly telling him that he is stupid. Yet, sadly enough, there are teachers who do this repeatedly. Unfortunately, the child often believes the teacher, and if the idea takes root, serious psychological damage may be perpetrated. Many parents often make this cruel mistake. We should never insult our children, because insults are deeply, and often far-reachingly, painful.

Confidentially

Michael once told his teacher, quite confidentially, that he longed to be an artist—so much so—that he often "fibbed" about pictures which he traced and said he had drawn. So far as the teacher could see, the child had no ability in drawing or painting—but he had a definite way with words. His composition work was a delight.

The teacher's response to the child was this, "But Michael you *are* an artist. You do make pictures, beautiful pictures! Not with crayon, or water color, or paint, but with words!"

A few months later, Michael ran up to his teacher to show her his poems in the school magazine. She beamed at him, thinking, "He doesn't realize I submitted them." Years later, to her delight, Michael returned to visit. He is now a high school English teacher.

You are in a position to make every child stand tall, to nurture his self-pride and to build his self-confidence—the first step toward success.

Individualized instruction for the sick child

So often, children have illnesses such as heart ailments or asthma, which go virtually ignored by the teacher. Individualized instruction for such children is of paramount importance—indeed it can be a matter of life and death.

Let us first look at the cardiac child. How much more important it is for him to learn how to take care of himself than for him to learn the new math. Speak to the child's parents and to the school doctor. Find out what the child needs to know about his condition. Then, give him detailed instructions, so that he will be habituated to health habits that may prevent him from having a heart attack.

The cooperation of the entire class may be enlisted in helping the sick youngster to maintain good health. You will find that most of the children in your class will be eager to cooperate in helping the handicapped child. The teacher should impress upon each member of the class that it is his responsibility, too, to help the affected youngster to function as normally as possible.

The same type of individualized instruction should be given to the asthmatic child, the diabetic, the epileptic, or the child with an ulcer. Enlist the cooperation of both the school doctor and the school nurse.

The obese child, so frequently found in our classes today, needs help. He should be taught the basic rules of nutrition, of exercise, and of how to control the compulsion to eat. He may need to find a substitute for eating—by sublimating. If you are able to help him find an activity he enjoys—such as sculpting or metal work, painting or playing a guitar—perhaps he will be able to diet. If he does lose weight, applaud him—but privately. He is easily embarrassed, and often, highly sensitive.

Neurotic, moody children, too, need specialized individualized instruction. Try seating them near youngsters of more wholesome temperaments. Talk with one of the latter children privately, saying, "Mary Ann, I know you're a happy person. You have such a lovely disposition. I'm going to seat Janie near you. I know, with your cheerfulness and your sympathetic nature, you'll try to make her feel happier, too." The child usually responds eagerly and very helpfully.

You can give the children lessons in mental hygiene which will hopefully help give them a happier and more wholesome outlook.

Individualized instruction in regard to his illness, is for the sick child among the most important educational experiences he can ever have. Of course you don't want to overdo it, lest you emphasize the illness unduly. Yet the awareness you build up, and the health habits you help him inculcate, will serve him—and lengthen his life.

This individualized instruction for the sick child can be done at any grade level, considering of course, the child's level of understanding and maturity. Do not burden a little one with facts that will frighten him. Stress a positive, rather than a negative approach. As a child gets older, he is able, of course, to comprehend more. He will probably be everlastingly grateful to you for "leveling" with him.

In using individualized instruction with sick children, and with their healthier classmates, you can develop feelings of compassion and of belonging to the family of man. The times in which we live make this tremendously necessary. Do not be afraid to approach the topic of illness, for children are often exposed to it at home. The sick child, and his classmates too, need to know how to handle emergencies. Your work in this area is teaching material of the greatest value in terms of the children's daily lives. Be careful, however, never to embarass any child—because children can be very, very sensitive.

Summary

In considering the basic psychological needs of children, we must first realize the tremendous importance of building a positive self-image. Individualized instruction helps us to do this, because we are able to suit the work to the child's particular abilities. We can show him his responsibilities and that we expect him to do well. When he requires teaching, we can teach him what he needs to learn. This enables him to have feelings of accomplishment. These should be stressed and emphasized by rewards—trips, commendation cards, and parties.

Individualized instruction is the tool we have to teach children what they need to know to live successful lives. We should extend this type of teaching to the sick child—helping him to learn health habits he needs to function and live a normal life.

4

How to make time for individualized instruction

There is no question about it! You must actually create the time to do individualized instruction. You will need to structure your class; and to plan your lessons with this in mind. If you are going to be able to work with each child, and give him the attention he needs, and the work he is capable of doing, you will have to have the other youngsters gainfully employed. They will need to develop good work and study habits. However, if they do so, you will have taught them a great deal. How many children graduate from elementary, and even from high school, with no idea of how to study? Consider the time you spend on developing work and study habits to be an investment in the children's academic future.

There are many time-saving devices. In this chapter, we shall discuss a number of them. We shall also go into many types of work which children should do independently.

Establishing routines

There are excellent reasons for establishing patterns of behavior, which are referred to as routines. Foremost is that most children are more comfortable with established patterns of behavior than without them. Routines do not have a negative effect on creativity. Quite the reverse is true—because the day-to-day chores are taken care of almost automatically.

The routines you establish will have to suit the children. If they do not, it is almost like wearing clothes which do not fit.

Write out the routines you are establishing step by step. There is no reason you cannot read them, later, to the children. List each detail. This is far easier than answering questions. Then, let the children write them in their notebooks.

Here are some basics: Complete them to suit your class.

1. Lining up.
   Where.
2. Going up to class.
3. Entering the classroom.
4. What to do if teacher is not there.
5. Sitting down.
6. Hanging up clothing.
7. Talking until teacher signals for attention.
8. Getting ready for work. Cleaning desk.
9. Sharpening pencils (when and if).
10. Starting work.
11. Procedures for speaking.
    (Do you want children to raise hands, or do you prefer they speak out?)
12. What to do when work is completed.
    (a) Using library corner.
    (b) Using art corner.
    (c) Using science corner.
    (d) Using newspaper or magazine corner.
13. Moving on to other subjects.
14. Routines for terminating the day's work.
15. Children's responsibilities.

Teach the children *exactly* what you expect of them. Repeat the same directions for several days. Have youngsters discuss them, but make sure the children have them "down pat." Practice the routines the first week.

The routines will be the key to giving you time for working with individual children and with small groups. They will prevent much disorder—so that the individualized instruction can be given without being marred by noise or confusion.

Entering the classroom

We suggest you select six children as sergeants. These should be chosen from among the physically large youngsters, and should be among those who have shown a sense of responsibility. (Check the record cards if you wish to select capable children before you really get to know them.)

If the children get on line in the yard, give each child a specific partner. If the partner is absent, the child stands alone. (This last item is important because it prevents arguments.) Try to avoid having close friends as partners to prevent chatting. You may wish to place a well-behaved youngster with a mischievous one. Place two sergeants at the front of the line, two at the back, and two in the center. The rules are: the children must come up in an orderly fashion—without running, without pushing, without fighting—and if it is the policy in your school, without talking. Use this system for dismissal as well.

If your children don't line up to enter the building, use this system for dismissal every single time they have to leave the room. Make each and every dismissal a "fire drill." Explain the seriousness and the importance of this daily drill so that, in the event of a fire, tragedy can be avoided. Also emphasize, again and again, that no talking, pushing, shoving or fighting is tolerated during dismissal—for each dismissal is a rehearsal in the event of a fire.

To prevent any confusion have your class artist make an attractive chart headed, "Our Places During a Fire Drill." Then list:

1. Mary and Bobby (Sergeants)
2. Alice and Jack
3. Thelma and Alex

Have the chart made large, colorful and attractive. Hang it in a conspicuous place in the classroom.

The children must be made to realize this is very serious business—that any infraction of the law of the fire drill endangers everybody's life. More people are hurt because of screaming and pushing than by fire.

By using each dismissal as a practice for a fire drill, you

inculcate safety habits and, at the same time, you make your life far simpler, and you prevent accidents.

Establish this routine from your first day. Make up your mind you will not tolerate any disorder—and don't. Should a child give you trouble, get in touch with his parent. What parent would not understand the importance of the fire drill?

Seating arrangements

Never allow your children to sit anywhere they wish. Seat them! Have a blank seating chart, and after you've given the children seats, place their names on it yourself.

Check through the children's health records, and seat any child with a visual or auditory problem at the front of the room.

Leave several seats near your desk unoccupied. As you get to know the children better, you can use these seats for the children who require your special attention—or you can use them as rewards.

It is important that you seat the apathetic or hostile child near the front of the room. These are children who need the special stimulation you can offer to them. Misdemeanors are often prevented this way. "The watched pot never boils."

You may wish to seat an apathetic child with a bright child who is interested in schoolwork. His interest may become contagious. Or try seating a poor reader with a good one. Should you have a child with a health problem, such as one with a cardiac or other ailment, seat him near a gentle child, one easy to get along with. Never seat a sick child near a hostile or a mischievous one.

Ronald was a child who had had open heart surgery. Another boy, named John, was a great one for practical jokes. One of his favorites was to shout "Open Chest." If the youngster he shouted it at did not fold his arms to protect himself, our joker would hit him in the chest.

Ronald wisely said to his teacher, "Could you talk to John—and ask him not to play 'open chest' with me? I'm glad I don't sit near him. He does it to those kids all the time."

The teacher had been completely unaware of John's behavior until Ronald had the intelligence to speak to her about it.

If you have plants, and you can easily, choose a child who has a "green thumb" for your plant monitor. Seat her near the window where she can take care of the plants, and report on their growth to the class.

You may wish to assign the role of class host or hostess. Seat this child near the door. His task is to welcome visitors, after opening the door for them, and, when they leave, bid them goodbye, and again open the door for them. These little attentions will promote an *esprit de corps* and a nice atmosphere in the classroom.

Hanging up clothing

Select a clothing monitor, and seat him near the wardrobe.

Assign a hook to each child, and have the monitor label it with the youngster's name. (Give the lower hooks to the smaller children, the upper ones to the taller.)

It is also the monitor's task to open and close the wardrobe at the proper time. It facilitates matters, and prevents confusion, if the children hang up their clothing row by row, with the wardrobe monitor presiding.

Keeping the room clean

In this area, too, the children can be of tremendous help. Select two housekeepers—one who is naturally tidy, and one who could profit by this type of assignment. Sometimes, the little girls may like to bring aprons.

The housekeepers are in charge of tidying the library corner, the science corner, the art corner, the window sills. You may even trust them with tidying up your desk. Have them make a final inspection tour of the room, every afternoon before leaving.

Assign a basket monitor to the task of taking the basket around the room five minutes before lunch and five minutes before dismissal. Desks should never be left with papers or other litter in them.

An inspection of the desks should be done periodically by the housekeepers. If anyone defaces a desk, it should be reported, and cleaned by the pupil who marked it up. This will discourage them from repeating this offense.

The housekeepers see to it that all supplies are put away in the closets.

The children, in this way, are encouraged to take pride in the appearance and cleanliness of their room. Do not hesitate to try this approach with any grade level. Even 7th graders will eagerly do these tasks.

Individualized responsibility

What could be more important than teaching children responsibility? So often we neglect this elusive sense; many teachers fail to take practical steps in this direction. Furthermore, if handled well, the children will welcome responsibility. If handled unwisely, they will withdraw from it. Particularly the problem children will benefit by having responsibilities entrusted to them.

Ann is a fighter. She'll fight at the drop of a hat. The reason may be that she is the youngest of eight children, and she is pushed around by the seven others.

She was a very difficult child to have in class. She always had an angry look on her face.

Her teacher found life with Ann getting to be unbearable, and went for help to the guidance counselor.

After they discussed Ann for awhile, the counselor asked, "Could you possibly make her some sort of monitor? Not after she's done something horrendous, but early one morning before trouble arises."

They agreed that Ann could keep the blackboards clean. She was to be in charge of washing them, (why do they love this job so much?) of removing dust from the tray, and of erasing the boards whenever necessary.

The teacher would have tried almost anything. This task had a quieting effect upon the child. She seemed, after a while, less hostile—and even smiled occasionally.

Rules for individualized responsibility

1. When you assign monitorial tasks, do so for a finite period— such as one to two months.

2. Make sure every child has an assignment.

3. You can use the threat of removal as punishment for poor conduct. The threat is far more effective than the deed—and easier for you. However, if a child insists upon behaving antisocially, then temporarily, at least, remove him from the job.

4. In a private discussion with him, you might assure him that if he proves worthy of the trust, the job will be reassigned to him.

5. Your object in this should be to make the child feel important. A sense of responsibility is born, and the child's self-confidence is nourished.

Here are some individualized responsibilities to which the children will react favorably:

Sergeants for fire drill— already mentioned.   (6)

Housekeepers. (2)

Attendance monitor—who records the names of absent pupils on the board.

Homework monitor—gives absentees homework assignments.

Distribution monitors (2) hand out papers, pencils, etc.

Collection monitors (2) collect materials, tests, etc.

Class officers (4) (elected, with great responsibility.)

1. President—takes charge of class when requested to do so.

2. Vice President—takes charge of class when President is not available.

3. Secretary—writes letters, keeps notes.

4. Treasurer—collects money.

Plant monitor.

Fish tank monitor

Blackboard monitors (2)

Host or hostesses—greets visitors, seats them. (Seated near door.)

Chalk monitor—keeps trays supplied with chalk; cleans dust off trays.

Shade monitors—adjust shades.

Pencil and pen monitors (2)—see that every child has these—lend them, and make sure they are returned at end of day.

Class librarian—in charge of class library.

Wardrobe monitor—opens and closes doors—keeps wardrobe clean.

Supply monitor—carries supplies to classroom. Puts them away when they come.

Out of room monitors (2)—go on errands.

Any other monitorial job that you find you need is suitable.

Often the children will suggest a job for which there is a need. These usually work out very nicely.

How can you get this to function well?

1. Emphasize the importance of each job, and the fact that the work is being done by everyone in the class participating—so that no one (including the teacher) is overburdened.

2. This cooperative effort on everyone's part fosters an *esprit de corps* in the classroom. The job is accepted by the children with eagerness. Hostile behavior is discouraged.

3. Pick jobs suited to each child's abilities. If a child is allergic to dust, don't make him the blackboard monitor.

4. Teach each exactly how to do his job. Then, when the time comes to change jobs, have each train his successor.

5. You may wish to post a sign with the tasks listed, and the children's names indicated on it. (Make all posters attractive. Use plenty of color.)

6. If you find a child unsuited for a job, change it. Don't try to fit the youngster to the job.

Routines which save your time and that of the children

1. Always have work on the board for the children to do when they enter your classroom. This is excellent procedure whether you are teaching in the first grade or the twelfth. It settles the children down, and establishes the pattern for the day. The work can be review or practice; it might even be new work or work that requires opinion. But its presence on the board helps you. (Don't use work below the level of the children's intelligence—so called "busy work!" The latter may have a negative effect on the children.)

2. Always have work for the children to do when they've finished the assignment you gave them.

Time is precious. Never permit it to be wasted. Reading or even looking at magazines or newspapers is worthwhile. If you have library, art and science areas set up, the child can select an activity which meets his needs at the particular time.

3. Establish the routine that, when a particular bell rings, it is time for all talking to cease, and for work to commence. If this pattern is established, it can save you and your class thousands of minutes.

4. If a child is disruptive, try to discover why he is not doing his work. Every teacher has heard the excuse countless times, "I have no pencil." Or pen—or notebook. Have supplies available, lend them to the child who needs them, but then, "Let's go. Come on. Get started, please."

The child may not know how to begin the assignment. If this is his problem, you can easily solve it.

Explaining the system of individualized instruction and how it works

The children should understand the system of individualized instruction and the goals. It is worth the time and effort you spend to make it clear to them. We suggest you cover the following points:

1. The outstanding goal is that each child try to accomplish as much as he can. He will be on his own a good deal of the time. He will sometimes be the teacher—working with weaker students— teaching them subjects in which he is stronger.

2. Students must learn self-control if they are to gain from the individualized instruction. A relatively quiet atmosphere should be maintained in order to promote thinking.

3. In individualized instruction explain how you will be working, sometimes with one, and sometimes with another child. There will be times when you will be teaching a group of children, and at other times the entire class will be involved. If every child understands this, cooperation may be taken for granted.

4. Stress a feeling of unity. The class is one family, each member contributing for the good of the whole. This may be

pursued when children teach other children, or when you ask them to bring in materials. It can be extended to party making, assembly programs and such occasions as Field Days. (Field Day shouldn't be neglected—for here is the healthfulness of the outdoors, combined with fun and games.)

A Field Day need not be a school-wide affair. Classes can enjoy it, individually, or you may wish to get together with another teacher or two. Friendships are often born on Field Day. The lonely child might find a friend on just such an occasion. Very often children can get closer to the teacher, and can confide in her under these conditions. They become garrulous—often discussing their lives and problems at home and in school. The teacher is able to learn much about her youngsters, which she cannot do as well in the formal atmosphere of the classroom.

5. The parents, too, should be given an understanding of this new approach to learning, and their cooperation sought.

Parents should be instructed in how to help their children at home if they wish to do so. It should be emphasized that at all times the children should be *encouraged* to work, and never discouraged. A derogatory parental tone will do much to defeat the child, and make his progress slower. It can also have a devastating effect on his personality.

In speaking to the parents, if you can convince them to be kind and patient and gentle with their children, you will make a great contribution to the children's happiness.

Parents are too apt to criticize their children adversely. This is a serious mistake and one of the chief causes of the generation gap.

6. Explain to the children that at times they will be marking their own papers.

Experience has taught us that, in the actual process of marking their own papers, children learn a great deal. Furthermore, you can save a great amount of time.

Discuss the correct answers, and the reasons for them, while the marking is going on. If you feel there is a need to do so, you can eliminate temptation by following a simple rule. The children take a test, using pens. Then all pens are put away, red pencils are taken out, and the marking proceeds. Not only does this teach the correct answers, but in the computation of the rating, the lesson also becomes one in functional arithmetic.

Teaching children to teach other children

First, introduce this system by announcing "This technique can only be used with very mature children. If you feel you are not mature enough to handle it, please let me know." It is a rare child who will admit he is not mature enough to handle a situation.

Second, spend some time training the little pupil teachers. Make sure they know exactly what it is they are to teach, and exactly how they are to teach it. Of course, you will choose only those children who have an adequate grasp of the subject matter to be taught.

Emphasize the point that a good teacher is a kind teacher.

Try to give every child an opportunity at sometime to assume the role of the teacher. Incidentally, this is a beautiful way of introducing the teaching profession to children. Do they have a propensity for teaching?

Make this a very fluid situation. The child good in arithmetic may teach it. The child who reads well may help the poor reader. The good baseball player can instruct the others in this sport, which many of them love so well.

Switch teachers around. Don't assign one child to another permanently.

It's up to you as the teacher to show all human beings have strong and weak points. We should never be ashamed to reveal them, for it is only by making them known that the weak points can be strengthened.

Helene is a brilliant musician who has performed at many concerts. She maintains that today she cannot add a column of figures accurately, although she is an adult, because, during her childhood years, she was ashamed of her weakness in arithmetic.

Research and group work

Two of the most important techniques you can utilize to enable you to work with individual children are assigning research projects and having your children do group work.

Even fourth graders are capable of doing research on topics within their comprehension. When a child looks up information, he is required to read. He can use pictures, but only to a limited extent. Social studies is a favorite area for research; give the youngsters specific subjects within this area. For example, if you are studying the world, allow each child to select a country to learn about. Have reference materials in your library corner so that the boys and girls can work within the classroom. Of course, they can also use the school library.

You may wish to use children's magazines. Select several articles and/or pictures and design a series of questions for the children to answer, after having read the article.

Have them do research on health habits, finding out as many important ideas as they can in regard to their personal health, the health of other children in the class, and everyone in the community. (They may also send to various health organizations for posters, pamphlets, pictures and information that is relevant to this subject.) Using the material they've learned, they can compose a play for Health Day, compose songs and poems and do posters on the subject.

Older children can do much valuable research and then construct plays based on what they've learned. A historical play can be developed by the youngsters after they've read a biography of the characters. For example, you might have them study Elizabeth I of England and her half-sister Mary, Queen of Scots. This story had wide appeal and would interest both the children and an audience of their parents if the play were presented to them.

Research may involve children working alone or in groups. The latter has certain advantages. Leadership qualities are often developed, and the children's imagination is sparked.

If you wish to have them work in groups, you must realize the room will not be quiet. This type of noise is wholesome, for it is indicative of intellectual activity. The freedom afforded the children is also desirable provided the noise doesn't become too loud.

However, all group activity must have a purpose. You may assign a topic for discussion. The results of the discussion should be reported back to the entire class. This method is excellent when you want the children to contribute ideas.

This is group work, not group teaching.

Very often work, well done by a group, can be taken up by the entire class because the children in the group have become enthused, and their enthusiasm is contagious. In the case of the work we mentioned, Elizabeth and Mary, it became a class play in which every child took part. It was presented for graduation, with sinister parts omitted. It included songs sung by Mary's songster, poems and the reading of historical documents. One of the most moving moments of the play was the reading of an actual letter written by Mary to her half-sister, pleading with Elizabeth to spare her life, and the lives of some of her friends.

Building a success pattern for every child

You can actually make time in which to do individualized instruction, and build a success pattern for every child by giving the children assignments which bring out their talents and their creativity.

Here are some of the types of work you can assign:

1. Drawing and painting abstractions.

In order to help your children succeed in this, you must assist them to develop ideas. For instance, if you tell a child to draw a picture to bring China to mind or of Chinese objects, he may be able to do this—or he may not. But if you discuss the subject first, by asking "What do you think of when I mention China?" And list the subjects on the board, you give him ideas to work with, and to help generate his own ideas.

China? Brings to mind tea and silk, and the Great Wall, and dragons and chow mein, fortune cookies, Marco Polo, Hong Kong, fireworks. (These items were listed by a fifth grade class.)

But, you're asking, how can the children build a success pattern? They can't draw. The clue here, the key word, is abstractions. Encourage the children to strive for representation, not realism. If you can recognize the items, fine, but recognition is not necessary.

When else can you use this technique? Read a description of a scene, and have the children draw an abstraction of it. The same can be done with a story, or an event, a holiday or a famous person.

Stress the use of color, and encourage the children to be free.

2. Allow the children, at certain specific times, to "do their thing."

Put a list of activities on the board and allow them to choose the ones they prefer. These might be activities involving one, two, or a group of children. They could include using the art materials, the science materials, the reading corner. They might work with wood or wire, clay or cork.

3. Give bonus academic assignments. Allow the children to work on them in pairs or groups.

These may be serious assignments or "fun assignments." For example, an assignment such as What time is it in:

London
Sydney
Istanbul
Fairbanks

Los Angeles, etc. is both serious and fun. So is Find a partner for each of the following:

Adam and _____, George and _____.

You would vary the questions according to the age level and the sophistication of the students.

You can develop a file of these assignments, and keep a record of those completed by each child.

Other types of assignments involve vocabulary development:

How many words does the dictionary have starting with aq; what are they? With pn, etc.

Or "How many words can you find in transcontinental"? How many words to you know beginning with "pre," or ending with "tion?"

Team teaching

The system of team teaching was developed to utilize the talents and interests of teachers to the utmost. It can, also, serve as a method for conserving teacher time—so that this time may be used to do individualized or group instruction.

Check with your supervisor. If there is another teacher teaching the same grade you do, is it possible to have the two classes meet together, for class instruction? This might be for a social studies lesson or for a science demonstration. It could be for literature, or music. While one teacher is teaching (and she might be assisted by paraprofessionals), the other is free to do individualized instruction with one child, or with a group.

Team teaching is a relatively new method which is effective for the presentation of material. If there is more than one class on a grade, doing the same level of work, the classes can be put together, and taught by one teacher. They then break up into smaller groups for discussion and work.

This method may be used for individualizing instruction relatively easily. While one teacher is teaching the large group, the other teachers may be working with individual children, or with small groups of youngsters having the same needs.

Team teaching is a time saver, too, in that only one teacher is required to do the large lesson planning, freeing the others to work with the children in need of individual help. The large group may also do written work, thus further increasing the amount of time available for individualized instruction.

Summary

In this chapter, we have concentrated on techniques you can use to help you find time for individualized instruction. The establishment of routines is very valuable because you don't have to repeat the same instructions day after day. Once the children have learned them, you are freed, for the most part, of this chore. Many areas of behavior should be routinized: the class entrance into the classroom, their seating arrangements, the manner in which they hang up their clothing, the way they keep the room clean. You can approach these routines in a relaxed manner, for, once established, they should hold. Individualized responsibility teaches your children many things—among them self confidence.

Your children should be taught the value of education in general, and of the individualized instruction program in particular, if they are to get the maximum benefits from it. They can be taught individually by you, by other adults, or even by their fellow students. However, by helping them to learn, and to feel successful, we move them forward on the road to learning. Individualized instruction can prevent children from feeling defeated, and build a self-respect they desperately need.

5

Teaching self-control–the

essential ingredient for a

successful individualized program

Mrs. Z. is a teacher's teacher. She has devoted a great deal of time, thought and energy to refining the individual instruction program in her class. She has spent many hours preparing materials and lessons. One day she told us, "Two of the children asked for permission to sit in the hall and read. And, you know, I'd like to move my desk out there. Everyone is working beautifully–but it does get noisy in here." Mrs. Z. is eminently successful–but we'd like to make some suggestions which would make her a bit more comfortable. Noise is uncomfortable, and can have a very definite physical and/or psychological effect. The problem is to cut it down. Some buzz is essential, but it should be considerably below a roar.

Having the children establish rules

When individuals are involved with the law-making processes, they tend to be far more willing to accept the laws than if they are thrust upon them. Consequently, even with the very young children, as well as older ones, have at least one class session devoted to setting up rules and regulations.

Do this after school has been in session for about two weeks, so that the need for the rules is evident. Make this rule making session an important occasion. Announce to the class in advance, "On Friday," (or whenever you wish) "we will be in *legislative* session to establish the rules and regulations under which we will function." Treat the matter with respect and convey this feeling to your children. The day before, repeat the request that everyone come to school, in order to have his or her say in this very important matter.

Use the words, "legislative" and "legislature" even with second graders. This is vocabulary building done with relevance. The legislature in Washington or your state capital is far away. In your classroom, legislation can become a real thing.

On the appointed day, early in the morning, announce, "We are now in legislative session. As you know, it is the legislature which makes the rules. Let us get started."

If the class has already elected a president, allow him to function as the class leader. If not, elect a leader for the day. The secretary and the treasurer can both take notes, the former on the board with assistance from the latter.

Tell the class there are many areas which require regulations. Here are a number for consideration.

1. Entering the classroom.
2. Putting away clothing.
3. Using the classroom materials and resources.
4. Using one's voice.
5. Working with other people.
6. Cleaning up after work is completed.
7. Putting materials away.
8. Reporting problems to the teacher.
9. Running around in the classroom.

Have the children suggest one or more rules to cover each situation. The secretary then writes them on the board, and the class copies them. The treasurer may write them on a rexograph for duplication, or the youngsters may copy them into their notebooks.

In this situation, as in all classroom situations, hostility must be avoided. Rules should be worked out, after being discussed back and forth. Encourage as many children as possible to give opinions. You may wish to have the rules voted on—as a bill is voted on in Congress. But try to get the children involved. Children become enthusiastic, and it is hard to curb their enthusiasm—but this is the purpose of these rules. Call on those boys and girls who do not volunteer. Get their opinions, too. Be sure to involve those youngsters who are going to be discipline problems. Make every effort to show them they are important and that their opinions matter. The time you spend on this can be most worthwhile. Sometimes children don't understand why rules are necessary; your teaching should include the reasons.

One way to do this very dramatically is with role playing. Say to a child, "Give me your radio." (or pen or whatever valuable object he may have.) Say it with hostility so that his reaction will be "No." If it isn't, go on to another child. Shout, "You can't have it. I'm not giving it back." Get highly emotional until you elicit the response, "She (or he—meaning the teacher) can't do this." Then you ask, "Why not? What protects you? Why can't a person take your things?" Get at the idea that laws are made to protect all of us, and to make it possible for us to live together compatibly. The classroom should be a society in microcosm— with each of us contributing to it.

Distributing copies of the rules

After you have developed rules it is important that you distribute copies of them to the children. You can do this in one or a variety of ways:

1. Probably the best way is by having them copy the rules after you and the class have developed them. This gives them experience in writing, which they need.

2. You can have the rules written on a rexograph master and duplicated for distribution. Have the children place the rules in their notebooks.

Ask one child who is good at printing to make a poster stating the rules, and display it in a prominent place. When you find a youngster is breaking a rule, you can readily call it to his attention.

Make the rules a part of life. Don't write them down and forget them. They can be a very important tool, if used properly, but they must be enforced. If a rule has been established that a parent will be called by telephone if a child gets into an argument, you must telephone. If the rules are ignored by you, they certainly will be ignored by the children.

Making children familiar with school regulations

Besides the rules made in the classroom, there are school regulations with which the children should be made familiar. These, too, are important tools for you. Give the youngsters copies, if they are available, or place them on the board for copying, but distribute them. This permits you to take action, without being accused of being unfair.

A respect for rules and regulations, at this time in the development of our nation, must be inculcated in our children. By so doing, we give them a structured situation, which helps develop a sense of security.

In individualizing instruction a certain amount of freedom is essential. Children must be able to move about in the room and work in different areas. You need rules to keep the voices down, and to avoid running in the room. Both are important. Establish these rules at the very beginning and be sure the children realize that they will be enforced. This makes the difference between an environment in which children work, or one in which everyone gets a headache.

Using the school handbook

If your school has a handbook, the rules and regulations will be included. Seeing them in print is a valuable experience for the children. The printed page often carries more weight than word of mouth, particularly with youngsters.

If you can, obtain a class set of handbooks and use them as the basis for a lesson. Cover all of the material in them, but stress the rules and regulations aspect. Again, the purpose of this is to keep the rules in the children's minds.

If your school has no handbook, perhaps you and your class can work on one. (This is an excellent project for fifth and sixth graders.) Check with your supervisor to find out if such a book is needed. If it is, the production of an actual handbook can be a very exciting unit. Individualize the work by giving each child a task he can accomplish successfully. It may help to obtain copies of the handbooks of other schools to serve as guides.

Children respond to your expectations of them. The school handbook should be based on this psychology. It should stress positive rather than negative behavior, and should place responsibility for his behavior on each child.

In individualizing instruction, if you use this psychology, you will find most of your students will respond favorably to it. Children, as a rule, do well when they are given responsibility, providing they can handle it. We will base many of the activities in these pages on this principle.

Establish rewards and penalties

One of the ethics on which our society is based is the concept that fine work is rewarded. You can use this very effectively in your teaching. Rewards take many forms: grades are the most common, and the most important. *Never give a child a failing grade.* Show him how he can improve his work. Have him do it over again. If he cannot do it correctly, review it yourself, to make sure it is not too difficult for him. Help him—until he earns a good mark.

As you work with him, encourage him to try to do better. You may assign another child to work with him or you may ask his family to do so. However, gear the work to his ability, and teach him as you go along.

In addition to grades, we should try to inculcate in the children the idea that successfully completing their work is its own reward. Feelings of satisfaction in a job well done are emotions well worth developing. A sense of accomplishment is achieved.

What other rewards can you offer? Parties or trips are excellent. Neither need be a very big thing. Soda or apple juice and a cookie and you have a party. A visit to a local pet shop or aquarium store, and you have a trip. Trips, particularly, are educational as well as rewarding to the youngsters.

Rewards should surprise the children, but penalties should not.

Set up your penalties, with the children, long in advance. Do this when you establish the class rules. Make sure that each penalty you establish:

1. Is one you can carry through.

2. Is not too severe. It's very important that the punishment fit the misdemeanor.

3. Is one you will pursue. Don't ever threaten to do something and not do it. The children lose their respect for you, if you do.

It is most important that you show fairness in all your dealings with children. They are quick to note partiality, and they lose their regard for a teacher who is unfair. Not only that, but they lose confidence in her, too. A teacher should make every effort to give each child a square deal. Should it be necessary to give some children more attention than others—and this is often the case—the situation should be explained to the class, preferably when the child in question is not present.

Is there any adult who does not remember another child who was the "teacher's pet," who ran all the errands, and to whom the teacher often addressed her remarks? And isn't this a memory which lingers and rankles? This type of attention is unsalutary for both the class and the child involved. It sets the child on a pedestal, can make him extremely self-centered, and give him an exaggerated idea of his own importance. In an unwholesome way, the other children are made to feel inferior.

It is easy to fall into a pattern of dependence on one child—or on a group of children—and neglect the others. So often, it is the bright ones who get most of the benefits of the teacher's attentions, and even instruction. This is, of course, ironic. Like carrying coal to Newcastle, those who need it the least are getting the most. In a word, the bright child will learn with or without a teacher. It is the slower learner, the shy child, the reticent one, the youngster with the least intellectual security who should be given the greatest share of instruction and attention. Let us nourish the intellectually impoverished!

Every teacher has many tasks to perform. Having youngsters assist is a great help to the teacher. However, avoid having one or two children carry out many duties. As we have outlined in a previous chapter, every single child in the class should have some task for which he is responsible. In this way the work of the classroom is fairly divided. No child is being slighted.

Perhaps, you may feel this assignment of monitorial duties is a bother, but the contrary is true. If you put the time and effort into assigning duties for each child, your endeavors will bear fruit. In the long run, you will find yourself relieved of many time-consuming, irksome duties.

Establishing class teams

One of the best means of helping children develop self-control, as well as an *esprit de corps,* is by establishing class teams.

You may divide the class into groups for arithmetic or for spelling. Have them vie with each other. Set up friendly competition, and make the drill work come alive. Allow the children to elect the team leaders, and then have the leaders select the teams. First one leader chooses one child, then the opposing leader chooses one child. This is done until each child in the class is placed on a team. Or, you can have a boy's team and a girl's team.

Have the children select a name for their team, and even a team symbol and a color. You may make armbands with commercial felt, which is inexpensive, and felt pens. The art department can help, remembering that any assistance that you obtain from them motivates their work.

You may use the band as an incentive. A disorderly child cannot wear his band. He doesn't get it back until he behaves himself.

You can also have charts made indicating the winners of the team tournaments. Your only limitation is your creativity. The teams may have arithmetic matches, spelling matches, or vocabulary matches, and the same techniques can be applied to any subject area.

Class officers

Lessons in the democratic process should be a most important part of your educational program. The classroom can be a living democracy.

Two or three weeks after school starts, have the children elect class officers—a President, Vice President, Secretary, and Treasurer. It is up to you to train these children. Give them duties and teach them how to perform them. If you do not give the children authority, you do not give them training in leadership. They need this to succeed in this highly competitive world. Allow the officers, at some specified time during the day, to take charge of the class, while you sit on the sidelines. You may wish to do this early in the day, when the class is most easily controlled. Of course, if an officer misbehaves, he forfeits his position and a new election is held. Be sure that this rule is established and understood.

Your class officers should be a great help during a fire drill—and should have been trained beforehand. They must know just what to do and where to go. If you prepare them for this work, your task is far simpler. You have four people helping you.

Working privately with the children who have problems

Individualizing instruction in terms of helping children adjust to the society in which they live is critically important. You need not do a lesson with the entire class, if one youngster has a problem— but you should help *him* to solve it. For example, the child who loses his temper must learn to control his anger. He should be taught to bring his grievance to his teacher or the class president, but not to take matters into his own hands. The child should be shown the two points of view—his own and his adversary's. The teacher may ask, "How would you feel about this if you were Jimmy?" (Jimmy is, of course, the child's adversary.) This should be discussed by the teacher with patience, and with an understanding of what it means to have a "hot" temper. The teacher should listen carefully to what the child has to say, and try to show him that reasoning should take the place of emotional outbursts. In this way, self-control is initiated.

If a child shouts out, he should be taught to ask himself, "Why am I shouting? Is the reason I'm doing this important enough to disturb the class?"

When a child has few friends, and does not get along well with others, teach him to listen to other children, and become interested in them and their lives. A lonely child needs help desperately. The loners are among our saddest little ones, and are usually very, very vulnerable. By your attitude of paying attention to this child he gains status in the group. Other children, sometimes, will accept him. This is what we want to happen, of course.

You can even work with the obese child, teaching him to substitute a low-calorie bit of food instead of his usual high-caloried snack. When he wants to eat between meals, tell him to substitute some activity he enjoys. Perhaps, he might draw or play ball or do some physical activity. He might even sing or play a guitar. In this way, the child learns to substitute one state of mind for another.

Another problem is the hyperactive child. His need for physical activity can be solved by giving him the messenger assignment. However, if there aren't enough messages, give him physical work to do. Cutting pictures from magazines for collages is a possibility. Take the child's interests and talents as a basis for the activities.

Trips

We mentioned trips as rewards. They are far more than that. They are educational experiences in the world outside the class-room.

Trips are a perfect time to build rapport with your youngsters, and to listen to their problems. This is particularly true of the child with difficulties or the one causing difficulties in the classroom. Encourage him to talk about himself. This is sometimes difficult with non-verbal children, but far easier on a trip than during other circumstances.

During a trip you can get an idea, often, of what a child's home life is like. We are amazed at how frequently we discover serious financial and spiritual problems, which we had no inkling existed. Very often they stagger the imagination. The child might have a drunken father, or a sadistic mother. Some of our children have older brothers and sisters who are drug addicts, and this can very easily affect them. Use the intimacy of the moment to elicit the child's problems. Sometimes help can be obtained for them. The rapport we mentioned before, with children having specific problems, can more easily be done in a trip situation, where informality is the keynote, and where the child's problem is disclosed only to the teacher. Confidentiality should be assured. Handling problems in this manner may preclude bursts of temper, and help the child to control himself—especially if he feels that in his teacher he has found a friend.

Summary

If people did not learn self-control, we would live in a state of chaos. Self-control is one of the basic facts of surviving, essential to a successful life in our society. Adults cannot do anything they feel like doing. Nor can our children. It is one of our tasks to teach our boys and girls this self-control.

Establishing rules is far better if done by the teacher and the children, as partners, than if made by the teacher alone. Be sure that each youngster has a copy of the rules, that he understands them, and that he believes they are fair. This last point is extremely important, for you will refer to it time and time again. Children should be aware of the school regulations as well. It is essential that both rules and regulations be feasible, and that no statement is ever made which will not be followed through. Individualized instruction is impossible without appropriate, carefully thought out rules and regulations which are put to use.

Expect your children to live by these rules and regulations, and tell your pupils that you expect them to do so. Encourage them, always, to develop self-control. Use a reward system to foster good work, and good behavior.

Use class teams to develop an *esprit de corps* within your class. Elect class officers, and teach them to function in these roles.

Individualize your instruction by helping those children who need help in adjusting their behavior to that of our society—both in your classroom and in the outside world. Use trips as rewards, and as a chance to develop rapport and even to instruct those children who have problems, or who just need your attention and concern.

Self-control is not a by product. We must help the children—particularly the disruptive children—to understand what a tremendous asset this power is. We must teach self-control as a very important concept, remembering that without it, teaching anything is well-nigh impossible.

6

The key to teaching
every child to read—by
individualizing instruction

Using a constant series of diagnostic tests is the essence—the essential to the successful teaching of reading.

In individualizing instruction, the very basis of your teaching must be diagnosis. This must be a continuous process; without it you are teaching in the dark. The number of children who have no idea of how to approach a word they do not know by sight is unbelievably large. In standardized testing a child may have scored 3.0 on the Metropolitan Achievement Test. If he was taking an advanced form, he got the 3.0 for writing his name on the paper. 3.0 indicates *he did not answer one question correctly.*

How can you tell at what level your children are functioning? First, try individualized testing for diagnosing comprehension. At the end of the first year, a child should be able to read all of the stories in the text. One simple way to test this is to have each child read aloud from the text. This is done on a one-to-one basis. You will be using the text and you can select any story for the child to read. Start at the beginning of a story (even the first one is suitable), and have the child read two pages. Then ask the youngster to read specific words in different parts of the page. By observing the manner in which the child reads, you can judge whether the youngster is actually reading, or if he has memorized the words. Make careful note of the errors he makes, since these will be the areas you will concentrate on in individualizing instruction.

Next question the child to determine whether he grasps the meaning of the material he has been reading. Include such ideas as "Who (or what) is this story about?" "What happened first?" "Why did this happen?" "Then what happened?" This type of questioning is necessary on every grade level, even the first. It is essential for you to know if the child is comprehending what he is reading.

Work up a check list of your own. Rexograph a copy for each child. As you have each child read to you, indicate on this list in which areas he is having difficulty. You will save time by noting the problems in this manner. This method will also make it simple for you to group those children who have similar problems.

This type of test is extremely valuable on any grade level. If you are teaching a fourth grade, and the child is unable to read a fourth-year story, try him with a third-year book. If he can't read that, return to the second-year text, or even to the first, if necessary. Has he mastered the sight words he needs to know? If not, indicate the ones he misses on your diagnosis sheet for him. What sounds does he read incorrectly? In other words, very specifically, where is he going wrong?

Remember, children are extremely self-conscious. While testing, you must be very deft, to avoid embarrassing the youngster. Try to praise him when he reads something correctly. Never, never allow him to get upset. Assure him he is going to learn to read, and that you enjoy teaching him. Get him to feel worthwhile, as a human being, and he will be far more receptive to your teaching.

Diagnosing progress in vocabulary development

Reading and vocabulary development are linked as closely as parent and child. In order to read and comprehend what he is reading, a child must know words and their meanings.

How can you find out whether the child you are teaching understands the words he is being taught? One method we suggest is by having a contest. Tell the children this will be a long contest, because you want to give them many opportunities to make points, and to show how well they can do. There will be prizes at the end. Give books as prizes, if you possibly can. This builds a love of them, and of reading. Be sure you select books that are colorful and attractive—the kind you'd like to win if you were the same age as your children. Check with your supervisor. There may be sample copies around which would be suitable.

Credit Staten Island Advance Photos by Barry Schwartz.

Figure 6-1

Distribute paper, have it folded in half, and numbered down the side. On one side, have the children list the words you dictate to them. (It is worthwhile to have them write rather than you rexographing this for them.) Then have the children write the meaning of each word in the column on the other side of the page.

For example, dictate the word "wise." Then suggest meanings— or have the children suggest them—but do this aloud, so that it serves as a sample. Place this on the board, to further show the youngsters how this is being done.

After you have covered the words you wish to cover in this

manner, call a halt. Give the youngsters a "seventh inning stretch." Then, using a new sheet of paper, tell the children they will be working in reverse. Make sure they know what that means. Then give them definitions, and have them write in the words. You may use words that were learned during the term in every subject area.

You may have the class work out this list of "words we have learned this term," with you. If you do this, do it several weeks before you plan to use it for diagnosis.

It is important to use words which can be defined easily. Try to use limiting definitions. A definition such as "the ruler of a country" is poor because many words fit that definition. "The leader of an orchestra" is good because the only answer is "conductor." If you cannot limit the definition, be prepared to accept any one which is correct. We guarantee your youngsters will come up with things you never thought of.

From this test, you are able to tell which children have not grasped the meanings of the words you have been using, as well as reading.

Diagnosing progress in reading comprehension

Prepare several paragraphs using the vocabulary from the material the children have been reading. Try to develop new thoughts with it, if possible, so that the children will not be bored. After they have read the material, have them answer questions on it—similar to those we suggested you ask orally. For the primary grades, your questions will be factual for the most part. As the children get older, ask more questions which require interpretation. You may take material from other tests or from texts for this purpose.

Here is a sample paragraph:

> We stood looking down three hundred feet into a living, seething, swelling, heaving volcano.
> We could feel its hot breath on our faces, burning our eyeballs.
> Our first look at the daily newspaper in Honolulu, when we landed, had informed us that "the volcano is erupting on the Big Island (Hawaii)." None of the New York newspapers had featured the story, or if they had, we hadn't seen it. But in February of this year, the volcano, Kilauea by name, which is located in

Hawaii Volcanoes National Park, erupted at the Mauna Ulu site, filling the air with a red glow, and the hearts of the people seeing it with joy and wonder, because these volcanoes are confined to their fire pits and are not dangerous.

We flew over to the Big Island from Honolulu, which is on the island of Oahu, then drove to the Park Headquarters. From there, we were directed to drive 11 miles along Chain of Craters Road. Next we parked the car, and started to walk. It's a mile and a quarter up hill. First there is a cinder path, through bushes and trees. Then we came to a place where lava had overflowed the previous year. We walked up and up until we were about 50 feet away from the top. Then we smelled it. Or rather, it hit us. Sulphur. We looked up at the sky, and we could see a red glow. We approached the overlook, and then climbed to the edge and looked down.

What we saw there we shall never forget! There it was below us, a sea of red hot, molten lava, in constant motion, as the ocean is when it is whipped by enormous waves. It flowed back and forth within its cauldron, back and forth—hitting the walls with loud splashes.

After the children had read the selection, they were asked to answer the following questions.

1. Where was the volcano erupting?
2. How did the author reach the site of the eruption?
3. How close did the author get to the actual eruption?
4. How can you tell the temperature at the site?
5. What did the lava in the cauldron look like?
6. What is a good name for this selection?
7. Why didn't the author know the volcano was erupting, before he arrived in Honolulu?
8. Why was it necessary to walk over lava to reach the site of the present eruption?
9. What is an overlook?
10. What is a cauldron?

When you find a child unable to answer a question, determine whether it is because he could not read the material, or did not understand it. If it is the latter, check to find the words he did not know. Be sure, too, that the child takes the punctuation into consideration.

Many school systems use standardized tests which are divided into word knowledge and reading comprehension. If your school uses these tests you can see by the results the level at which the child is functioning in each of these areas. A careful examination of this test paper, plus the oral reading test suggested at the beginning of this chapter can indicate to you in which skills the child is lacking.

Let us say a child in the fifth grade scores 5.0 on word knowledge, but only 3.6 on reading comprehension. When you test him orally, you find he recognizes most of the words, but is not able to figure out the main idea of the paragraph. He needs help in analyzing what he reads. This can be given by having him read paragraphs and then tell you "what they are about."

Other children have not learned the basic sight vocabulary, and need work on that.

It is vital to learn what, specifically, each child needs. This applies to bright as well as slow children. The bright may not lack skills, but can benefit from assistance in learning such skills as reading rapidly without error, or summarizing.

Working on reading, skill by skill

We can divide the teaching of reading into large basic areas. These will be elaborated upon later in this chapter.

Word recognition:
1. Through configuration clues.
2. By phonetic analysis.
3. By structural analysis.
4. Through clues found in the context of the material read.
5. By looking them up in the dictionary.

Children learn meaning:
1. By literal interpretation.
2. By comprehending the meanings implied by the words, but not explicitly stated.
3. By using critical judgment.

We must remember, though, that in order to read, a child must first be able to speak. Reading is translating the printed word back into speech, and then into ideas. A child cannot read and comprehend a word he has never heard before. (An adult may be able to do so, because he may be able to break up the word into component parts. A child cannot do so.) Children must, in primary grades, be given the meaning of every word they are being taught to read. This can be done by showing the actual object or verb (if the child doesn't know it), by showing pictures of it, by description or discussion.

Children learn words they can picture in their minds—nouns, verbs, adjectives, and adverbs. They have trouble with the seemingly innocuous words such as "of" or "if."

As you do your diagnostic testing, your objective is to find out which of the reading skills each child lacks. Let us say you realize a child is having trouble with "gh." You would refer him to the study material you have prepared for these letters.

How can you prepare such study material?

1. Use curriculum guides put out by your own school system, your state or college.

2. Use the programs provided by the publishers of the basic readers.

3. Check the various textbooks in the subject.

4. Use some of the ideas which follow. Once you prepare this material, do it on rexograph (dittos) and keep it on file, because you will find use for it again and again.

Telling a child a word is not teaching him to read. Reading is really decoding symbols to get at the ideas they represent. But the intermediate step, the words, must be in between—for the child to understand fully what he is reading.

WORD ATTACK SKILLS

Configuration clues

A printed word has certain characteristics, and a child may learn to recognize it by its appearance—almost by its shape. This is the configuration of the word. The child is told what the word is, and he associates it with the appearance of the letters. He does not figure it out, and he really can't be quite sure that he reads it correctly when he sees it again.

Configuration clues are used to identify only words that are already familiar to the child in sound and meaning.

When a child's reading vocabulary is small, and the words have distinctly different shapes and characteristics, configuration clues may be sufficient to identify those few words successfully. Most children, for instance, will learn the word "elephant" very quickly because of its configuration—the tall letter (l) following the first 'e', the 'p' going below the line, the 'h' rising above the line. This word has more individuality than the word 'an' which they do not learn as easily.

Young children often amaze their parents by learning product names from the television screen. Actually they are learning to recognize the product name by the configuration of letters plus other identifying characteristics the advertisers use.

Using a specific configuration clue will not enable a child to identify another word with the same clue.

Here are some of the most frequently used configuration clues:

Length of the word—a, at, ate
Double consonants—bull, class
Double vowels—root, tree
Tall letters at beginning of word—toe, he, tea
Tall letters in the center of word—she, shore
Tall letters at the end of a word—end, word, will
Letters below the line—eye, pen, go
Tall letters and letters below the line—stop, jewel
Capital letters—Mom, Dad, I
Outline or shape of word—airplane, elephant, television
Flash cards can be used to emphasize learning words by their configuration.

Have the children make their own flash cards. Index cards may be used and the words printed with felt pens. When a word is held up, the child who correctly recognizes the word and says it first gets the card. The youngster with the largest number of cards wins.

We have seen this technique used very effectively with 8th graders whose reading was on a 4th- to 5th-grade level. The words were words they selected from newspapers and magazines.

Configuration clues are basic in the development of the child's initial sight vocabulary.

Phonetic analysis

As you test your children, you will find some of them finding words they cannot read. They need some technique to determine what the words are. Phonetic analysis is one, very valuable method.

There are 26 letters in our language, but 45 different sounds. Learning to read involves learning the letters of the written language, the sounds of the spoken language, and the circumstances and conditions when particular letters and combinations of letters represent particular sounds.

We deal with two types of letters: vowels and consonants. Consonants and their sounds are usually taught before the vowels because the differences in sound are more easily discerned and because the appearance of the consonants is more distinctive. Think about the vowels. They are all small, roundish; whereas the consonants vary—tall, above or below the line.

In teaching children phonics, stress the identification and the ability to discriminate between sounds (and their letters). Next, associate the sounds with the letters and then blend them into words.

The commercial programs or teachers' guides for the use of the basic readers will supply you with material for individualizing your teaching in this area. A collection of these is of inestimable help.

Let us say in your diagnostic testing you discover a child does not recognize "boat." He doesn't realize the pronounciation of "oa" in this word. If you merely tell him "boat," you are not teaching him anything. Give him a work sheet with material like this to read:

> Billy was happy. "I am going out on a boat today," he said. He walked down the road to the boat house. A toad came out.
> "Mr. Toad, I'm going out on a boat," Billy told him.
> On the road he saw a goat.
> "Mr. Goat, I'm going out on a boat," he said.
> Then his mother called, "Billy, take your coat."
> "I don't want my coat in the boat." Billy said.
> Do you know what Billy's mother said? She didn't say, "You have to take your coat." She didn't say, "Be a good boy." She said, "No coat, no boat."

Billy asked, "Mr. Toad, do you think I need a coat?"

Mr. Toad didn't answer.

"Mr. Goat, do you think I need a coat?" Billy asked.

"No coat, no boat," Billy's mother said. What would you do if you were Billy?

1. Where was Billy going?
2. Whom did he meet first?
3. Whom did he meet second?
4. What did Billy's mother want him to take?
5. What did Billy's mother say?

Games with phonics

Have a child write a phonic element on the board. He is the "teacher." The sound, for example, can be "ee." He asks for words which have that element. Any child wishing to come up raises his hand. The "teacher" chooses the children and they each write one word on the board. The rest of the class copies the list into their notebooks.

A variation of this is to see how many words each child can think of—with a specific phonic element. Also, how many phonetic elements can the children list and build on. Think of as many games as you can to teach phonic elements and corresponding words.

If a child has difficulty with an initial combination of consonants, have him use his dictionary to see how many words he can find with this combination. For example, "kn." Have him list all the words he can find with "kn," then read them to you aloud.

Be careful to suit the material to the needs of the children. An older child will react badly to what he considers "baby stuff," in spite of the fact that he needs it. Plan your material so that he is not embarrassed by it. For example, an older child having difficulty with reading should read the newspaper and be helped with reading the words with which he is having difficulty.

Encourage him to try, stressing the idea that many of the words to be found in the newspapers are repeated. Children's magazines or sports magazine are another good source.

Since there are 45 sounds, you will need basic work sheets for each one. The work sheet must be on a child's intellectual level. A sixth grader could not use the material about Billy, Mr. Toad, and Mr. Goat without feeling ridiculous. A second grader would no doubt enjoy it.

For a sixth grader, your story might be about Billy going to the boat house; as he walked along the road he heard a moan and then a groan. The groan got louder and louder. Billy searched all over. In the trees he found a man who had been hurt. Billy covered him with his coat, and ran for help. What would you do?

It is most important to remember never to insult a child's intelligence. Furthermore, if you can make your worksheets relevant to the children's lives, they will become involved in your program because what they are reading applies to them. It is not only reading—it is living as well.

Structural analysis

Using structural analysis involves the recognition of parts of words.

For example, the words may have
1. Common roots
2. Prefixes
3. Suffixes
4. Inflectional endings
5. Compound words
6. Contractions

As a child learns more and more words, these should become stepping stones. For example, if he recognizes the words "air" and "plane" it becomes a simple matter for him to read "airplane"— provided he looks at both the parts of the word and the entire word.

All of the items listed above offer the same type of assistance. It is using a familiarity with words to be able to decipher new words.

1. Roots of words are often Latin or Greek in origin.

> graph—to write (from Greek "graphein")
> mobile—to move (from Latin "mobilis")
> idio—ones' own (from Greek "idios")
> psych—of the soul (from Greek "psyche")

2. Prefixes—a syllable placed at the beginning of the word which alters or adds to its meaning.

auto—"self"—added to graph—makes the word autograph—to write oneself.
im—added to mobile—becomes immobile—not movable.

3. Suffixes are generally added to a word to change its function and its part of speech. Adjectives become adverbs by the addition of the suffix "ly"; for example, badly, fairly.

4. Inflectional endings are added to change a word so that it suits the role it plays in the sentence. The meaning or part of speech is not affected; i.e., think, thinks, thinking.

5. Compound words are words put together. No change is made in either word—bathroom, sundown, pinfeather.

6. Contractions are root words put together, with some letters omitted; *cannot* becomes *can't, I have* becomes *I've*.

Structural analysis is a tool which every child needs if he is to be able to read fluently.

Teaching this area can be fun if you use a "games" approach. Make your work sheets worth points, and at the end of the month, or term, give a prize to the pupil with the most points. Then suit the difficulty of the work to the ability of the child.

You can work up a series of such worksheets or the children can compose them. *For example:*

1. List all the words you can find in your dictionary which start with "an."
2. Find all the words starting with "c" and ending with "tion."
3. List as many compound words as you can think of using as one part the word "school."
4. Find five words using as one part the root "tract."

Contextual clues

This technique involves having the child identify words by clues provided in the context of the material which he is reading. To be able to use this method, the child must have these words in his vocabulary.

A child should be shown that he can use the context to help

him—along with other techniques such as structural analysis or phonics.

As he reads, "The fox ran up the hill swiftly," he may not recognize "swiftly," but he can reason what the word might be. (To use this method, the reading material must be of interest to him.)

Children can be helped to realize that synonyms are often found in one sentence. For example, "She was intelligent, or clever, and this showed in everything she did."

Antonyms, too, often are side by side. For example, "For better, for worse, for richer, for poorer . . . "

They should be taught, too, that explanations are frequently added to fill out a sentence, and to make sure its meaning is clear. "The man was an Indian, whose family lived in Bombay."

Sometimes a child can discern the meaning of a word because it has been explained in the sentence. For example, consider the following: "The top soil had been removed by the falling water—a typical case of erosion." One meaning of "erosion" is explained, before it is found in the sentence.

All of these types of clues may be used in your individualized instruction. Again, work sheets may be prepared which will give the child practice in using these skills. The level of difficulty determines the material. A series starting with simple examples, and increasing in complexity, may be developed over a period of time.

These techniques are all valuable in the teaching of word recognition. Everyone of the word attack skills should be taught to each child—so that he has many ways, at his disposal to figure out what a word is. Please remember, though, that if the youngster has never heard of the word, never met it in conversation, he will have a very hard time of it. For this reason, before covering new material, make sure you introduce him to the words, so that when he meets them again, they will at least be acquaintences, if not friends.

Teaching reading comprehension

In teaching reading comprehension, we begin with literal comprehension, then go on to interpreting meanings not stated in so many words in the selection, and finally progress to evaluation or critical thinking.

1. Literal comprehension

This is the simplest form of comprehension, requiring the least amount of thought.

Who, what, when, where? The answers to these questions, and to others which require literal comprehension, are relatively clear, and obvious.

2. Interpretation

To interpret, the child must be taught to take the facts in the selection he is reading, and to reason with them. To teach interpretation, you must discuss with the children exactly how they go about this. Let us take into consideration this paragraph:

> José lived in a warm, sunny country. The olive trees grew in rows and rows outside his window. He loved to open his eyes after his siesta and look at them.

What thought processes does a child go through to answer the simple question "In what country does José live?" To teach this, first you might ask "In what country or countries do people name their sons José?" If the children know the answer, tell them to keep it in mind. Even if they do not, tell them they are to listen to the next clue. "Which of these countries is warm and sunny?" And still another clue—"Where do olive trees grow?" And then the last clue, "In which country do people take siestas?"

By answering these questions, the child is led by association and reason to find the answer to the original question "In what country does José live?" Point out, too, that they could possibly get the right answer from only one clue—that they did not need all of the clues, but they are there to help. Many of the standardized reading tests use this type of question very frequently.

3. Critical thinking.

Critical thinking requires a personal reaction: and that the child bring some knowledge to the paragraph he is reading.

For the short selection just given, what might a child reply to the question "Why don't we take siestas in the United States?" The paragraph tells the reader the weather is warm and sunny. If the child has learned about the siesta, he will recognize it in the reading selection, and apply what he knows of it to our country.

He might also be asked, "Would José's family cook with olive oil? How can you tell?"

This aspect of reading is not simply recognizing and pronouncing words. There is far more involved.

To teach this skill, review paragraphs the children have read, and ask them questions which are not answered directly by the selection, but which have to be thought about first.

In individualizing instruction, it is important to work on all three aspects of comprehension. For your own edification, study some of the standardized tests to see how children are tested. Then work out your own paragraphs, with questions for the children to practice on. Use questions with literal comprehension, interpretation, and critical thinking. The last, of course, is the most sophisticated, and will require the most ability on the part of the children.

Teaching each child, or grouping those with similar needs

When you have done diagnostic testing with your class, you will probably find some children with similar needs. Others should work individually.

1. Make up your groups according to the specific skills the children must learn.

If three youngsters need work in recognizing basic words, have them in one group.

2. Keep these groups flexible. As soon as a child masters a skill, have him move on to another area.

Some teachers group children according to their reading grade levels, and then keep them there indefinitely. This can have a defeating effect upon the child.

By moving the children into and out of groups, and by showing them they are able to learn, you are able to contribute to their self-worth. This is tremendously important.

3. You can have a child teaching another child. Children learn while they teach, for the tutor benefits as well as the youngster he is tutoring. However, be sure the child teaching is not going to lord it over the "pupil" in the situation.

If you use students as teachers, be sure you give exercises to do—so they know exactly what they are working on.

Credit Staten Island Advance Photos by Barry Schwartz.

Figure 6-2

"You will be working on the different sounds of the double o," you tell the child-teacher. See how many words you and Mary can think of. Look through your book with her. Be sure you pronounce each one. For example, "door" or "roof" or "boot." Can you hear the difference? Does the child who will be teaching? If not, how can he or she teach it to another?

Assigning reading gives you time to work with each child

In order to individualize your instruction, you must have time to work with each child. To do this, and to have children working to raise their levels of achievement, many teachers prepare material. "Contracts" are one form of this. Another method is the reading conference. The child is permitted to select a book or is assigned one, depending on which the teacher considers the best move at the time. The youngster sits down and reads it—in class;

he then selects a card which has the questions he is to answer. When he has answered them, he puts his name on the list the teacher has requested the children to write on the board. The teacher has a conference with him, going over the questions, and once a month having the child read aloud.

With children in the fourth grade or above, you can use several copies of specific books and hold group conferences instead of individual ones. However, this does not eliminate the need for hearing each child read aloud frequently.

When you build up your library for this type of individualized reading program, use books on a wide variety of reading levels. Encourage children to try books above their usual level—assuring them that it is desirable for them to experience difficulty with words occasionally. However, stress to them the need for learning to read and to understand each word as they encounter it.

Give children time to read in class. This will, in turn, give you time to individualize your instructions. However, be sure the material you have for them is of interest to them. This is most important. Set aside one to two periods a day for this work. You may find your children require more. If you are able to give priority to reading (depending on the philosophy of the school in which you teach), you may want to use the full two periods. Don't allow the children to get bored. This can be avoided in a number of ways:

1. Allow a group to put on a play.
2. Allow the groups to play charades.
3. Have each child give a talk "selling" the book he read to the rest of the class.

The meanings of individual words, of sentences, of paragraphs, and the message of the entire selection should be covered during every single reading lesson. This can be done by having children paraphrase the material. Sometimes, the story lends itself to dramatization, and this is particularly effective for enrichment.

Questioning brings out meaning. Have some children ask the questions, and others answer. One game is to have the child who answers ask the next question. The action is kept going in this way.

You may also have a child draw a cartoon or a picture, or suggest a picture with a few lines. Then someone else writes the definition under the picture.

Making reading a pleasure

1. When children have mastered the elementary reading skills, encourage them to read many books. It is essential that you have a class library. There is a plethora of excellent reading material available. Don't ask a child to read something he doesn't care for. Allow him to find something he enjoys.

The children should select their own stories, books or poems. After they have finished reading them, hold a conference to discuss the material read. Question the child to determine whether he understood it, and if he had any difficulties, to determine where they were.

One youngster was given a copy (an old one, unattractive and discolored) of *Julius Caesar.* She was assigned a number of pages and told to read them quickly. Her teacher found her, instead of doing this, reading *The Blue Fairy Book* under her desk. It was a beautiful, clean book, filled with colorful pictures. She'd taken it from the library.

Absorbed in the book, the youngster did not see the teacher approaching, and the child was yanked to her feet and dragged to the front of the room. "Look at this great big girl reading a baby book instead of Shakespeare," the teacher commented. Do you wonder that the little girl was turned off? Of course, no teacher reading this would ever do anything as obvious as this, but it is easy to imagine a teacher saying, "Aren't you a little old for this sort of thing?"

2. Display attractive books! Open them, and allow the children to peruse them. You will be surprised by the children's requests. We've heard youngsters who apparently had no interest in books suddenly say, "Could I have this one?" What would you answer? One clever answer was, "Of course you may borrow it—if you can show you deserve it." (This, of course, if the child's conduct is questionable.)

3. Children, even older ones, love to be read to. However, this should not be too frequent an occurrence. On some occasions, you can have your children do the actual oral reading. After any such activity, be sure you question the children to teach comprehension skills.

4. You can have a "question bee" by having a selection read aloud, and then having the children ask questions of one another.

5. Take the young children to the public library. If there is a "story hour," allow them to take part.

Encourage them to join the library. Use a large colorful chart to list the names of the children who have joined. Also, have the children bring the books to school and read aloud to their classmates.

6. Make reading aloud (for young children) a privilege. "Who wants to read to us?" Don't force a child to read. Allow those who do to select their own material.

7. Use children's magazines and newspapers. Keep even old copies on hand, for the children to read when they have completed their work.

Reading races

Children often enjoy competition. One way in which you can use this very effectively is by holding "Reading Races."

Have a large number of books, on all grade levels, on hand. Have a large index card with a series of questions for the child to answer when he has finished the book. These may be answered orally or in writing.

Make a large chart, with each child's name listed. Print this attractively. Leave room for each child to read many books, and for each he has read (and answered questions) place an indicator next to the name. You can use flags, stars or circles.

Encourage the children to read at home as well as in school.

Mrs. W., the parent of a college freshman, returned to visit one of her child's former teachers. "I just want to tell you," she said, "that Rosemarie read more books while she was in your sixth grade class than she has ever read in a year since. Your reading races did it!"

The more enthusiastic you are, the more the children will read! The better your introduction, the more they will clamor for the book you are talking about.

Summary

We are sure that it is unnecessary to stress the importance of reading to any teacher. No child can succeed academically without this skill.

How can we most effectively teach our children to read? One way is by individualizing instruction. To do this:

1. Do diagnostic testing to find out what specific skills the child lacks.

2. Teach word recognition by configuration clues, by phonic analysis, by structural analysis, by contextual clues, by use of the dictionary.

3. Teach comprehension first by literal comprehension, then by interpretation and then by critical evaluation.

Work with each child to meet his specific needs. When several youngsters have the same need, they may be taught by grouping them together.

Try to make reading a pleasure, to get the children involved in reading and unafraid to try even what to them is difficult material.

7

Teaching the language arts skills every child must have

Establishing goals

In order to live in this "civilized world," one must be able to communicate with his fellow-men on a sophisticated level. We teach communication whenever we teach, regardless of subject matter. However, it is stressed in the language arts. The four areas of communication are listening, speaking, reading and writing. We have already discussed reading, and now let us devote ourselves to the other areas.

Whenever you teach skills, in order to teach effectively, you must do diagnosis and then individualize your instruction to meet the needs of each child. Therefore, it is necessary to develop diagnostic tests for spoken and for written English.

However, before we consider the diagnostic testing, let us think about our goals. We will begin with oral or spoken language. This is tremendously important, you will agree, and yet it does not receive the stress it should, in many language arts classes. It is an area we almost take for granted—and we cannot do so. We must place emphasis on language usage from the time the children enter our schools.

The goals which follow have been adapted from a series called

English Language Arts, published by the State Education Department of the University of the State of New York, Bureaus of Elementary and Secondary Curriculum Development. They are given according to grade levels. We have tried to make them as practical as possible.

How to teach the use of our language

From kindergarten to third grade, each child should learn the following skills:

1. To understand the concept of desirability as it applies to social activities of all kinds. This desirability is in terms of dress, behavior, equipment usage, and language usage.

Our children can readily see, for instance, how undesirable it is for an adult to eat spaghetti with his fingers. The children must be shown how undesirable certain language is—in specific circumstances.

2. To recognize there are differences in pronunciation in different parts of our country. ("You all," spoken by a person whose speech reflects a New York upbringing, does not sound the same as when it is said by a Texan.)

3. To understand the regional standards of pronunciation. (A child who speaks with a New England "twang" is as much entitled to do so as one who speaks with a Western accent.)

4. To understand that correctness is a matter of usage. Teach the children to be aware of the variety of ways of saying something—and of the need to express themselves correctly. For example,

> I don't have anything.
> I don't have nothing.
> I don't got anything.
> I got nothing.
> I don't got nothing.
> I haven't anything.
> I have nothing.
> I ain't got anything.
> I ain't got nothing.

Discuss with the children which of these statements are correct, and by repetition have them learn which are not correct, or, in other words, which are not desirable.

5. To recognize the various levels of usage. There are some words which are nonstandard, and therefore not generally accepted.

This is a point which must be handled carefully, yet cannot be ommitted, if we are really educating our children.

In grades four to six the skills to be taught are:

All of the above.

6. To understand that there is a need for an American English standard language, and that this standard is important to learn.

Point out to the children that one's use of the English language may help or hinder him throughout his life. The need to express oneself well cannot be overestimated.

Use examples of speech from all over the country to bring out some of these points.

One of the important aspects of this set of aims is that you can refer to it each time you correct a child's speech. When someone uses a word which you prefer not to be used in class, immediately question it—on the grounds that it is not desirable, or that the child is hurting himself by not using standard American English, and that you don't want him to do that—*to himself.* You aren't criticizing the child, but instead are teaching him standard speech.

It is our feeling that unless we teach excellent use of the language in our classes, where will our children learn it?

List these objectives on a large chart, post it, and refer to it frequently. When a child uses a word which the rest of the class should learn, call it to their attention—as being good standard American English.

Give the children examples of excellent speech, and help them to achieve it, themselves. Individualize your instruction by having each child select a series of words, and teach them to the entire class. (Review the words with the child-teacher before doing this—just to be sure he knows what they mean, how to pronounce them, and that they are appropriate.)

In grades seven through nine these skills are suggested:

a. To recognize that usage is a matter of desirability and social acceptance.

b. To recognize there are different levels of usage.

c. To recognize that each of us has command of several levels of usage.

At this point, you will notice there are only three goals. Please remember, though, that if there is a need to return to lower levels because the children have not mastered those skills, it is essential that you do so.

How can you teach these skills, and reach these objectives?

Here are some ideas which should help:

1. Set up a number of hypothetical situations. Have the children give responses to remarks, choosing those which they feel are most appropriate, and those which they feel are not. Have them justify their choices.

You might have them read or perform portions of "My Fair Lady," which brings out the points particularly well.

2. Have the children do role playing, to show how they converse when with their parents, their teachers and with their friends.

3. Have the children hold conversations "on the telephone."

Young children enjoy making phones, using two juice cans and heavy cord. Have the youngsters stand at either side of the classroom and speak.

Older pupils, too, need this practice. When a person speaks on the telephone, he must enunciate particularly clearly.

Check with your local telephone company. There is equipment which certain companies make available to the schools. One example of this is the "teletrainer," which is composed of two phones, with an instrument box. It functions and sounds like a real telephone connection.

4. "Guess who I'm talking to." This is a game. Give the class a topic. Have the child say a sentence—and let the rest of the class guess to whom he or she is speaking—parent, friend, classmate or teacher. Have each child do this. Point out the differences—that speech among peers is far less formal than with other people.

Grammar as a living force

Grammar is one of the most misunderstood of all subjects. Children must be taught it—if they are to use the language correctly. Yet grammar has been obscured by cloudy thinking on the part of many teachers. We are going to give you a series of goals, by specific grade levels. As you read them, you will see that they are simple, to the point, and, most important of all, they cover the essentials a child must know. They do not, however, include a great deal of extraneous, befuddling matter.

In the first year teach:

> The sentence.
> The statement.
> The capital letter at the beginning of the sentence, and the period at the end.

In the second year, teach:

> A review of the first year's work.
> The question.
> The imperative sentence.
> The use of the question mark.
> The subject of the sentence.
> The subject word of the sentence.

In the third year, teach:

> A review of all previous work.
> The exclamatory sentence.
> The use of the exclamation point.
> The subject word and the predicate.
> The predicate verb.
> The noun and the pronoun.
> The agreement of the verb with the subject word—for example, when to use is, are; was, were; have, has, etc.

In the fourth year, teach:

> All previous work.
> Object and indirect object.
> Adjectives—what they are, and when they are used.
> Adverbs—what they are, and when they are used.

In the fifth year, teach:

> All previous work.
> The preposition.

The phrase.
The conjunction.
The adjective phrase.
The adverbial phrase.

In the sixth year, teach:

All previous work
The infinitive.
The participle.
The complete sentence, as opposed to the phrase, or the run-on sentence.

In making grammar come alive, we suggest you do the following:

Have the children list all common errors, and explain why they are incorrect. Take a scientific approach—*why* is important. Perhaps in this way, they will all remember that "them books" is wrong, because "them" is a pronoun, and cannot be used as an adjective.

Use the children's work. As you grade their compositions, copy their errors, and then write them on the board for discussion and correction. (Never embarrass any child by attributing an error to him.)

When you need examples, get them from the children. In teaching adjectives, have the youngsters list as many as they can. Do the same with any part of speech. Then add some of your own—to build their vocabularies.

You have a curriculum, of course, which will help you in selecting work for your children, but keep this listing in mind, too, for these are the "musts." If a child masters this amount of grammar, he will be able to use our language successfully, and incidentally, it will help him in the study of foreign languages as well.

Spelling, capitalization and punctuation

When a child has learned to read a word, he often has learned to spell it as well. However, there are many words he never learns in this manner. In our study of language arts, spelling, capitalization and punctuation must be taught. Your best sources for these areas are your curriculum guides and textbooks. If a child has not learned these skills while in the lower grades, he should be taught them in whatever grade he happens to be.

We have found spelling is taught, but punctuation not as often. Again, use the children's work as the basis for your lessons.

Spelling

1. Diagnostic testing.

You will be using syllabi for this. Pre-test the children, starting with a syllabus two or three years below their level. Determine which words they did not learn. Then assign to each child those words he spelled incorrectly. Arrange to test him individually on just those words. You may, if you wish, have the children work in pairs, first, and then "test" each other. Then, as a culmination, you give the one big test, with all of the words—whether they were missed by one child or all. Teaching the words from the lower-grade syllabi is very important. So often a child will never learn to spell "receive" properly because he never learned it in the grade where it was first taught, and no teacher, subsequently, taught it to him.

2. Many teachers are still using the pretest-test method in which a pretest is given on Monday, the children have the week to learn the words, and the test is given on Friday. The problem is often that the children know most of the words and can spell them correctly on Monday. If they are tested on them on Friday, what have they learned?

It is far preferable to concentrate on the words the child does not know, and to give him additional words to challenge him.

Give the children not ten words or 20, on a pretest. Give them 50. Then have them concentrate on all those they did not know. Collect the papers and have a monitor make a list of every word a child missed. Then, when you retest, divide the class into groups, depending on the words they did not know. Five groups or even four should do it. There will be some repetition, but far less.

3. Children still react well to spelling bees—once a month or

so—particularly if there is some sort of prize. (Even if it comes from the school stockroom.)

Tell the children they will first be given words they have studied, and then go on to more unfamiliar words.

4. Check a child's progress. When his spelling is very poor, work with him privately.

     a. Give him his own "challenge list."

     b. Motivate him to study it. The words may be relatively simple, but they must be learned, nevertheless.

     c. Teach him to study the words by:

         1. First thinking about each word.

         2. Then reading it aloud.

         3. Next writing it.

         4. Reading it again.

         5. Writing it again.

         6. Testing himself by trying to write it from memory.

         7. Having a parent or friend test him.

         8. Working with a tape recorder. He lists the words he must learn—slowly. Then he plays the tape back for himself—and writes the words. He then checks them against his list, and makes a new tape, with the words he still has spelled incorrectly. He repeats the process until he has learned all the words.

5. Have each child keep a graph of his progress.

6. Keep a folder of each child's papers for the parents to see.

7. Teach the children the words they misspell in their compositions. These are, after all, the words they are using—which they need, and which they should know. As you grade each child's written work, compile a list of words for him to learn. Be sure he learns it—or at least attempts to do so. Of course, you will have corrected the spelling errors in his composition as well.

Capitalization and punctuation

These should be taught using the same methods as those outlined for grammar.

Capitalization must, of course, be included when you teach spelling. There is no reason not to include proper nouns. In social studies, for instance, a child hears many names of people and places. It is worthwhile to help him learn to spell them correctly.

Developing diagnostic tests in written language

There are two types of test you might use to diagnose your children's written work. One is a review of the material you have been teaching. For this you can use short-answer or completion-type questions. If you have been working on the concept of the subject of the sentence, and its position in the sentence, have the children select the subject from a long series of sentences. Then have them construct sentences of their own, and select the subject from those.

Use this technique of having the children construct their own examples as often as possible.

Second, have the children write compositions. Tell them the compositions will be given two grades. They are separate and distinct. One grade is for ideas, thoughts, and the way they are expressed. The second is for the correctness of the written language. Point out that you want them to feel free to express their ideas, and that, at the same time, they must learn to use language correctly.

To get your children involved in this type of writing, give them ideas with which to begin. They need stimulation. Find topics that will bring them to life. This is not simple to do, but if you spend time on it, you will get excellent results. For example, decide on a topic such as "What would I do if I were the principal of this school?" Then ask the children who appear to be the most creative to place some of their ideas on the blackboard. Then ask for volunteers, and have them do the same. Try to get every child to volunteer. If necessary, inject some ideas of your own. When you have the board filled with ideas, tell the youngsters they may start to write any time they get an idea. Keep up the discussion until everyone is writing, and then start your work, individualizing instruction.

You can have writing done on topics the class is studying in almost every other subject area. Surely, social studies and science lend themselves to this work. Use the same concept—that the paper will be considered on two bases—content and language usage. The subject matter is almost unlimited. History, geography, current events, biography, explanations of scientific phenomena are some possibilities, but there are countless topics which can be the source of written composition. When you diagnose, look for spelling, punctuation, capitalization, and errors in grammar.

Finding time for individualized instruction

While the children are writing, you should use the time for individualizing instruction. Sit down with as many children as you can, working with them on their compositions. Look for those areas where they need help, and list them in your record book. (Develop a shorthand system of your own, so that you can work quickly.)

After you have seen all of the children's work, you are ready to make up groups or do individual work—based on the skills the children need to learn.

When you are having the youngsters write, and they have finished their compositions, have them go over their papers carefully. This is a habit well-worth cultivating. Many times they will catch their own mistakes.

If you need more time to complete your survey, you may have the children do over their papers again, this time selecting the subject from each sentence they have written. If they underline it with pencil (assuming the paper was written in pen) you can easily see their work, which will help in your analysis.

The time the children spend in writing is most valuable to them as well as to you. Therefore, do not feel you are overdoing this aspect if you have them write for 30 or 40 minutes each day. However, the lessons must be motivated, or the children will be unhappy.

Children enjoy writing fiction, provided they have a good starting point. Science fiction, spy mysteries, the type of material they often watch on television is a possibility. You may wish to allow them to explore their emotional reactions. ("How I feel when I am angry.") Favorite foods, games, friends, songs, movies, television programs, months, countries—almost anything may be experimented with—if you get a good response during the discussion period. Make sure that the children see that you are very interested in their ideas, as well as the written English they use. You may wish to have some children do autobiographies. This can be an on-going project, if you can get them sufficiently involved. Other children have worked on their "first novels."

Have every child make and keep up his portfolio. Use construction paper or folders, and give this collection importance by your attitude toward it. You will find you will be using it repeatedly to show the child's progress to him and to his parents, so we suggest you collect it at the end of each day, and keep it on file. If it is taken home, you will discover that it will get lost or, at the very least, become messy.

Individualizing instruction by bringing out the children's talents

Children often have talents which are not discovered, and never developed. We have found that one of the most successful means of finding such talent and nurturing it is through the presentation of a class production. One of the authors had this experience, as she prepared and presented a program on "Brotherhood Week." She had been asked to do an assembly program for the occasion. She took a vote, among her fifth graders, to select the story or poem they would dramatize. "The Elves and the Shoemaker" was selected. The children and the teacher converted the conventional story into a musical, at the same time making it a charming lesson in brotherhood.

The story was this: A poor shoemaker, a member of a minority group, and his family were in financial difficulty because his shop was not being patronized. The reason was that the shoemaker's religion differed from those of the people in the neighborhood. In the play, one day, Jim, the leader of the bigoted people, saw the children of the unfortunate family crying bitterly. Somehow, his conscience began to bother him. That night he fell asleep and dreamt he saw the little elves, but instead of making shoes, as they did in the conventional tale, they were dancing and singing songs for him. Here is one of them:

> Foolish ones, cast out your hatreds;
> They do you nought but harm;
> Giving birth to violence and cruelty,
> How they our hearts alarm!
> You and you and you are my brother,

> Whatever may be your race, creed or color!
> These are our words divine.
> Inscribed in our hearts in loving letters,
> They'll be forever mine!

"Who are you?" asked Jim.

"I," said the first elf, "am the spirit of love."

"And I," said the second elf, "am the soul of kindness."

"And I," said the third (he was the biggest elf of all,) "am the spirit of compassion. And would you like us to sing another song for you?"

"Oh, yes," said Jim.

"But will you promise," the third elf asked, "to listen with your heart?"

> Oh, list to a song we will sing for you,
> A song of love forever true.
> Our hearts are in trim, there are stars in the sky,
> Let us banish the clouds that hang nearby.
> Jew and Christian and Negro and White,
> Safe in our union, for love is our might!
> Soil our hearts never with hatred or fear
> All my loves draw thou near.
> Strong and staunch in our love evermore,
> Sharing our joys let not one heart be sore.
> Men will be brothers the whole world o'er
> Dwelling in love's sweet land!

As the play developed, many songs were written by the teacher and the children. In the end, of course, the bigoted child is won over, and then the other people in the community. And the shoemaker's family no longer has financial troubles.

The class was a bright one. Those youngsters who were musically gifted wrote the music, others with a talent for writing poetry, with assistance from the teacher, wrote the words of the songs, and the children who did well in composition revised the traditional tale.

Not only were the children involved, but the parents and community as well. The costumes were made by the children's mothers, and were incredibly beautiful. The crepe paper ones were discarded, happily. The children designed and made the scenery for the entire production. The play was given repeatedly at the request of the parents and then the community leaders. The spirit of love seemed to take hold of everyone involved. It was truly a memorable experience, and many children came away enriched because of the use of their talents, and because of the message.

How to work on specific skill areas

Just as described in the chapter on reading, you may assign work to the individual child—using textbooks, workbooks, worksheets, or contracts (a large, carefully delineated piece of work which the child is asked to complete.) You will, after he has completed his assignment, go over it with him. If you are fortunate enough to have a student teacher or a paraprofessional, he or she is well able to do this review, to help you ascertain whether or not the child has mastered the material you are trying to teach him.

When there are a number of children who are lacking in a specific skill, grouping them and teaching them is another possibility. If you are using this technique, encourage the children to ask questions, since if something is not clear to one of them, the chances are it is not clear to another—or even to the entire group. Tell them, "You are helping me to teach if you ask questions because I may not have made this clear to many of you—but I don't realize it until you tell me so."

Still another technique to use is to have students teach each other. Be sure you give very specific instructions to your "teachers." Impress upon them, too, that a good teacher is a kind teacher, and that they must help one another as they would wish to be helped.

Give homework to reinforce what you are teaching in class. However, if it even smacks of being "busy work," forget it. Homework which is not gone over the next day loses a major part of its value. You need not personally mark each assignment—the children can go over their own work—but you should spot check. If you don't, the chances are the children may lose interest, and be less conscientious about their work.

Parental aid

When a child is doing poorly, you should request the aid of the parents. By giving them specific instructions, and then reviewing the work after the child has done it, you can get much help—from almost every parent. Of course, there are some who are not capable of giving this assistance to their children, but you will find the large majority anxious and very willing. Be very careful to request the parents' assistance. Do not demand it. You might send home a note saying, "Dear Mrs. _____: I would appreciate it so much if you would work with Johnny on his assignment in English. He needs some extra help. I've given him this assignment. Would you do it with him? I shall be giving him extra work for the next few weeks. Can you help him with it?"

Teaching the art of sentence structuring

One of the most common errors which our children and subsequently young adults make is writing run-on sentences. This mistake requires much attention, if it is to be corrected. To best teach the structuring of sentences, use the children's work. If you follow the plan suggested above, you will have a plethora of material from which you can take examples. Even if you do not have the children write on a daily basis, you should have them write paragraphs two or three times a week.

Select sentences which are not structured correctly, and place them on the board. Have the class write them in their notebooks as they think they should be written. Then review the work with them. Have them explain why the sentence is incorrect, and exactly how they will correct it. As soon as the children are capable of writing paragraphs, they should be kept aware of the concepts of the complete sentence, and made aware of the errors involved in run-on (or incomplete) sentences.

Working toward more descriptive writing

Children need to learn how to speak descriptively. Their vocabularies need expansion. There are many ways to do this:

Write a noun on the board, and ask the children to write as many words as they can describing this noun in their notebooks.

Then make a list of their contributions on the board. Don't put a word on the board and have the children raise their hands to contribute. That is too easy—and the children who are reluctant to think don't have to bother. If every child must make a list, it will require more time, but the children all must make the effort.

Choose nouns which will stimulate the children to think. Animals are excellent for young children. Older children react well to sports, to games, to nature. Then go on to add concepts, such as love, peace, illness, comedy.

Continue this type of exercise with verbs. If the children cannot supply enough adverbs, you may want to give them clues, and have them guess the adverb. If they cannot guess it, teach it. Take the verb "run." What adverbs can the children suggest? Swiftly, quickly, quietly. But if they do not know these words, teach them to them. You might add stealthily, lightly, gracefully, gingerly.

Reading and writing poetry can help the children to learn much in the area of description. Haiku, the lovely Japanese form of short poem, is fine for this purpose. Limericks are good, too.

Vocabulary games for individualizing instruction

If your children have limited vocabularies, they may have a real need for new words. They can learn many in this way: Each child prepares a set of cards for himself. On one side of the index card, he writes the word. On the other side, he places its meaning. He develops a set of about 100 cards. Then he plays against himself to learn the meaning of every word for which he has a card. He looks at the word, and says the meaning. Then he turns over the card to check. If he gets the meaning right, he puts the card aside. He does this until he knows every word and its meaning. Then he reports to you. You will spot check, to see that he has learned the words. If he has learned them all, he should be rewarded with a commendation certificate or a small prize. Allow the child to tell you which words he wishes to learn. Perhaps they are from the newspaper, or from a magazine, from a book or even a television program. Encourage the children to select words they will use, and will be really proud of.

Vocabulary bees, similar to spelling bees, are good motivation. Tie these in with your teaching of reading and comprehension.

Crossword puzzles, commercially prepared, are considered games, but are a fine teaching device. Be sure they are not too difficult for the youngsters, because that turns them off very quickly.

Find a topic which the children can become involved in, and suggest each child discuss it at home, in terms of learning new words. Ask each one to have his family help him. Some topics you might use are "Words which come to our language from another language." ("Madam" is one example.) Words dealing with specific occupations, with medicine or law, with cooking or woodworking are all possibilities.

Have each child develop a list of words which he will teach to the class. The list need not be long—from six to ten words is fine—but, of course, it can be longer if the child so desires.

Some children need to learn to express themselves verbally

These are more often boys than girls. They often come from large families, where they don't get much chance to be heard. Whatever the reason, children must learn to speak. We have placed great stress on the need to learn to read, but the ability to speak is even more fundamental.

If you have children in your class who have not learned to communicate, they may have psychological problems. We would suggest that you refer them to the guidance department for counseling. Of course, you will be working with them yourself, as well.

This type of child will not do well in a discussion group, unless you structure the situation by assigning to each child within the group a specific topic. It can be a social studies topic, or a science one, but it should be narrowed down so that every youngster has a contribution to make. If the child needs assistance in preparing this contribution, work with him on it, so that he feels adequately prepared.

Another technique is widely used. It's called "Show and Tell." Each child brings in an object, and talks about it. The difficulty we have seen with this is that the reluctant speaker has nothing he wishes to talk about, or he forgets to bring the item in to school.

You may supply him with something, but if you do this, brief him very thoroughly. If this seems obvious, we apologize, but many teachers neglect to do this, and the child doesn't get to speak, even when most of the others do.

MOST IMPORTANT: ENGAGE THIS CHILD IN CONVERSATION. He needs someone to talk with him, to listen to him, to be interested in what he has to say. If it is you, the teacher, his ego gets a big boost. If you are willing to devote a lunch hour to him, or to her, because, of course, it can be a young lady, you will be doing a real service. Teachers are very verbal people, as a general rule, and it is hard for us to conceive of not being able to communicate. But we can also see how vital it is. A child who cannot express himself needs your help.

Learning the art of listening

Many more children need to learn to listen than to speak. Fortunately! And this, too, needs individual attention. The child who doesn't listen may, and probably will, grow up to be a terrific bore. He needs this art as part of his social development.

Try not to permit any child or children to dominate your classroom situation. This so often happens because we associate people who can express themselves well with intelligence. Where a child shows he is not willing to listen, work with him. Discuss the matter privately. You may find, as we have, that the child is not even aware of what he (or she, and usually it is she) is doing.

Lacey was the only daughter of two psychoanalysts. She was beautiful, bright and spoiled—and a very poor listener. She would have a comment to add to everything which was said, and her teacher found the situation becoming very difficult because the children were developing a dislike for Lacey, which was still hidden, but which the teacher felt would have to be shown sooner or later.

It was sooner. One day, in class, one of the girls piped up, "Lacey, will you keep quiet!"

The teacher could not allow this, of course, although she had known it would happen. She took Lacey aside, while the class was having physical education.

"How did you feel when Mary said that?" she asked.

Lacey did not look at her. She had no answer. The teacher continued, "You must have been very hurt."

Still no answer.

"Lacey," the teacher continued, "was Mary wrong?"

At this point Lacey burst into tears. The teacher allowed her to cry for a few minutes. Then she said to the little girl, "But Lacey, you've learned a very valuable lesson. Can you change?"

Lacey looked at her and sobbed, "I never realized I was doing anything wrong. At home I talk all the time."

Sometimes it takes more than one experience to help a child to see when he is at fault, but it is important that he realize that it is almost as necessary to listen as it is to speak. Sometimes more so.

Teaching handwriting, the almost forgotten art

So few teachers stress cursive writing today that our children are suffering from the lack of it—some suffering severely.

We are going to give you a method for teaching cursive writing, grammar and punctuation to little ones. It requires only a small amount of planning, but if you follow it, you will get excellent results.

This method is geared to the second or third grade. Plan on alloting 20 minutes per day for it. The children enjoy this work because it is very satisfying.

1. Begin by having the children fold a sheet of lined paper into four parts.

2. Make sure each child has a sharpened pencil.

3. Have lines on your blackboard. These can be placed there permanently, so that you don't need to redo them daily.

4. You will start with the letter "a"; begin with a discussion of it. "Do we always write the letter 'a' the same way?" you ask the children. Some will say no.

"How is it different?"

"Sometimes we use a big letter, and sometimes a small one."

"What do we call the big letter 'a'?"

Some child will know it's a capital.

"Now," you say, "let us write a capital letter 'a' on the blackboard."

You then write a capital letter "a" on the blackboard very

slowly, carefully, and beautifully. Because children are natural imitators, they, too, will write the letter slowly, carefully, and beautifully. On the same line, in the next column (the lines on the board have been divided into four columns, to correspond with those on the children's papers) you write another capital "a." Almost draw it, so that it is perfectly formed. The children will make a second "a," and they, too, will do it carefully because they are imitating you.

Now draw a third letter; have the children watch you and then do it on their papers. Finally, in the fourth space, you will again meticulously write the letter "a" making some remark such as "Let's make the 'a' look as if he drinks plenty of milk."

Let us assure you the children will form the letters beautifully if you follow this method.

Repeat this again, in the same manner on the next line.

Now we are ready for the small letter. Question the children, "What letter have we written?" They will reply, "An 'a'."

"What kind of an 'a'?"

Usually they will respond, but if they don't, ask, "What kind of an 'a,' a capital or a small one?"

Someone will say, "A capital."

Then you say, "Fine; now we can go on to the small 'a'."

Follow the same procedure for the small "a," writing two lines of the letter.

Next ask the class, "Is there any child whose name begins with 'a'?" If there is one, use the name. If not, ask, "Who knows someone whose name begins with 'a'?"

Let us assume you get the name "Anne." If you don't find an "a," say to the class, "My aunt's name is Anna. Let's use it—because it has two a's."

Now you question, "How shall we begin the word Anna?"

Some child will say, "With an 'a.' "

You ask, "What kind of an 'a'?"

Wait for the answer "It's a big 'a.' If it is not forthcoming, say to the children "Is it a small 'a' or a big 'a'?" Can you think of another way to say it's a big "a"? Someone will reply with the answer "A capital 'a.' "

Now pause, and say, "That's right. We use a capital "a" because you or I, your mommy or my mommy, your aunt or my aunt are very important. People are very important—so we begin their names with a capital. Who can spell the name Anna?"

If there is a child who can spell it correctly, pick this up and have the other children spell it aloud. If the child spelled it without saying "Capital 'a,' " ask the children to correct it. You will find the child will say, very dramatically, *"Capital 'a.' "*

Now write the word on the board, following the same procedure as you did with the letter. Write slowly, carefully and beautifully. You will find the children do the same. You are also developing a conscious sense and an awareness of writing and of grammar. You are bringing it to the focus of the children's minds.

We found the children very cooperative while a lesson of this type was going on. (They also knew that at the end of the lesson the teacher would write a large colorful grade, an "a," on the papers that were well written. They would immediately be hung up for display.)

We next move to the writing of a sentence. Ask the children for one. "Tell me something about Anna," you ask. It is surprising how often a child will say, "Anna ate apples." Then you repeat it. "Someone just said, 'Anna ate apples.' What did Anna do?"

Some child will repeat, "Anna ate apples."

Now you say, "When you told me this, what did you use?" Generally someone will answer, "We used words."

Ask, "What words did we use?"

A child will say, "Anna ate apples."

Then say, "That's right. When you tell us something—when you use words to tell us something, what have we got?"

Someone will say, "A sentence."

You will say, "That's right. We have taken some words, put them together, and told something. We have made a sentence. What is the sentence?"

The class will repeat, "Anna ate apples."

You ask, "How will we begin to write this sentence?"

"With a capital a," the children will answer.

"Do we have another reason for beginning with a capital?"

Someone will say, "Because Anna is an important person."

Write the sentence on the board, using exactly the same procedure as you did with the individual letters.

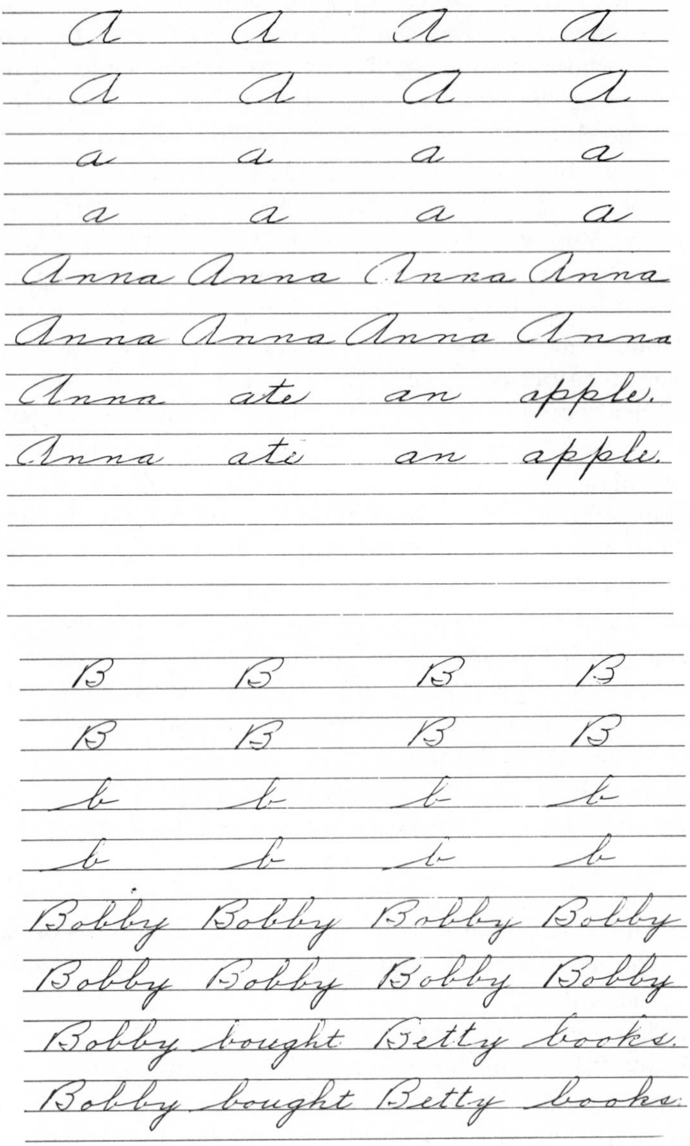
A A A A
A A A A
a a a a
a a a a
Anna Anna Anna Anna
Anna Anna Anna Anna
Anna ate an apple.
Anna ate an apple.
B B B B
B B B B
b b b b
b b b b
Bobby Bobby Bobby Bobby
Bobby Bobby Bobby Bobby
Bobby bought Betty books.
Bobby bought Betty books.

Credit Prall Intermediate School.

Figure 7-1

Have the children read the sentence. Ask them, "Did I forget something? What did I forget?"

Some child will say, "The period."

Ask, "Who would like to write the period?"

This brings a rush of hands. Have a slow child come up and put the period in, using colored chalk. (Have him select any color from the box.)

Now drill. Ask, "Why did we use a period?"

Then, "Why didn't we put a question mark like this?" (Write a question mark on another part of the board.) Let the children answer in unison, "Because the sentence doesn't ask a question."

Then ask, "What does it do?"

Look for the answer, "It tells us something."

Then you emphasize,: "Whenever we have a sentence that tells us something, we put a period at the end of it. Would you like to put a period at the end of your sentence? Do it in any color crayon you like."

Have the children write the sentence twice. Walk around the room reviewing the work. Put a large colorful "a" on every well-written paper. You will find a great many. Have the class president hang them up immediately at the end of each lesson. The results you get may amaze you. We have found this method to work very successfully.

Where a child cannot write the letter, work with him on an individual basis. Do not, however, belabor it. Have him write perhaps two lines of the letter, but no more.

Follow this method in teaching every letter. In like manner teach the use of the question mark, and the exclamation point. Commas, too, can be taught during this penmanship lesson.

You will find some children who will say, at first, "I can't." Perhaps they are the ones who are not as well coordinated as the others. At any rate, encourage them, work with them, but don't smother them.

The time spent (the 20 minutes suggested) is very little considering the work covered in sentence structure, capitalization, punctuation and spelling, as well as the penmanship. Also, you are making the children conscious of all of these areas—and as you will see, they enjoy it, and take an intellectual pride in it.

Please note that the children do not write the same words too many times. They learn to form the letters carefully and they are interested and enjoy doing so.

Enrichment for the brighter children

One of the obligations and advantages of the individualized instruction program is that it offers enrichment for the bright children. This, however, must be planned. It doesn't just happen, although many fine enrichment lessons grow out of classroom work.

Credit Official Photograph, Bd. of Ed., N.Y.C.

Figure 7-2

When you are planning your lessons, include special assignments for your brighter children.

1. These may consist of extra reading. For instance, you may have assigned *Huckleberry Finn* to the rest of the class, but your brighter children may have already read it. Have them select another of Mark Twain's books, to be read (as well as Huck Finn, if they haven't read it.) Perhaps, *A Connecticut Yankee in King Arthur's Court, Life on the Mississippi, A Tramp Abroad,* or any of Twain's other books. Follow this principle whenever reading is assigned. Also, offer credit for any child who reads, not the one book assigned, but additional books by the same author.

Have the children tell their classmates about these books, as well.

2. When a child shows an interest in a subject, have him do research on it. In class you may go off on a tangent. Have the child research one of these tangents. What are they, how do we use them, etc. The number of fields can be unlimited. Sometimes, you can structure this by introducing a topic to the class. For example, architecture. You show the class a photograph of the new skyscrapers. Who builds them? Why don't they fall down? When you get a good discussion going, you talk about an architect who wanted to construct a building a mile high. Who would like to do research about him? Any child who volunteers may then do some reading, and report to the class on Frank Lloyd Wright. Do not assign work of this type. Have the children volunteer for it.

3. Allow your bright children to prepare lessons, and teach them to the class. Give them specific instructions, though. Almost teach them to do a lesson plan, before they get up in front of the group. Most of all, make sure they have something worthwhile to teach, and teach them how to teach it.

4. You can have your bright children edit a class newspaper. Here, too, take volunteers. Allow each child who wishes to do so to participate. However, assign the editorial tasks to the children who are able to handle them. Give them the individualized instruction they require for this.

Make sure that the intellectually gifted children in your class are not overlooked. The techniques we have outlined are only a few, but they can "get the show on the road," as far as these children are concerned.

Summary

Even more than knowing how to read, a child must know how to communicate. Set up specific objectives in this area, make the children aware of them, and then work together toward them. Individualize your instruction to assist particularly the child who has difficulty in expressing himself.

Teach grammar to the youngsters in terms of speech and written language, rather than as exercises in diagramming sentences. Work out diagnostic tests in written language which stem from the children's own work, and from these determine wherein the children's difficulties lie. They will become evident from the written material. Use individualized instruction, then, to correct the errors the children make. Use it, too, to bring out the children's talents.

If there are a number of children making the same errors, group them and work with the group. If, after this reteaching, there are still youngsters having difficulties, work with them on an individual basis. If necessary, involve the parents in this program.

Teach the children to listen as well as to speak, to write as well as to read. For the brighter children, offer specific assignments which will enrich them, and which they may then contribute to the class.

8

Making sure no child is an arithmetic dropout

Arithmetic, a house of cards

The scene: a seventh grade mathematics class.
The time: the present.
The characters: Miss Smith, and 30 youngsters bent over their papers.

The class is working on problems in percentages. As Miss Smith walks around the room, she notices several children having difficulty.

"Is this right?" a little brown-eyed child named Tommy asks.

"No darling, it isn't," Miss Smith answers. "Let me help you." Miss Smith sits down to work with Tommy. She sees that he cannot master percentages because he cannot multiply. "5 times 8 is how much, Tommy?"

Tommy looks a little stunned. "30?" he asks.

"No," Miss Smith replies.

"33," he ventures.

"Tommy, you're guessing."

"38," he says, in a whisper.

Miss Smith says, "Tommy, 5 x 8 is 40. Can you remember that?"

"5 x 8 is 40," Tommy dutifully repeats.

What happens now is what tells the story of so many math dropouts.

"Tommy, you just don't know how to multiply," Miss Smith says. And then she walks to the front of the room, and says, "O.K. let's go over these problems. Let's help Tommy with them."

Tommy will never be able to succeed in doing problems because he has no foundation. Call it the multiplication tables, call it numbers facts, but whatever the name, how can a child learn arithmetic if he has not mastered the fundamentals. The study of arithmetic is much like building a house. Each brick you add depends on the rest of the structure. Oh, sure, a child can learn graphs, without basic skills, but he won't be able to figure out area, if he can't multiply. In the long run, he will be an arithmetic dropout if he has no foundation.

Diagnostic tests for every skill

More than in any other subject, arithmetic and mathematics require careful, constant diagnosis. Your class should virtually become a clinic. Let us show you how.

Spend time constructing your tests. Use textbooks. Begin with the one from the year the children have just completed. Take examples of every type of material—every chapter. Plan to spend a week or two on this testing. Make much of it. Tell the children, "This is an experiment. We are trying to see exactly where you are at. Which skills have you learned? Which are you missing? When we find this out, we can work out our arithmetic program together."

These tests are extensive. They should be done in pencil, because you are going to have the children mark them with pen. Rexograph the tests, and have the children divide the pages into 16 boxes. (Fold the paper in half, vertically, and in half again. Open it, and do the same horizontally. *Voilà*—16 boxes, 32 if you turn the page over.) When these are graded, it is a simple matter to study them and then to make your arrangements.

You have an average class. Some of your students will do well, some average, some poorly. But it is important that you find who is having trouble with what.

Give a number of questions in the same category. Let us say you are checking the children's ability to divide fractions. This serves several purposes. It shows up carelessness because if a child can handle the division of fractions, for example, he may make one or two errors, but he will get some of the questions right.

We suggest you give this test in stages. Thirty-two examples or problems per topic seem about right. Give as many examples as they can do in a day—and also correct them. Your children will work at different rates. Wait until three-quarters of the class has finished. Arrange your questions so that you have several of each type at the beginning, and then several of each type again and again. (Actually this is arranging the questions in layers.)

On the second day, while the children are taking the second part of the test, you can be studying the results (already graded by the pupils) of the first part.

Make a code, and prepare a chart:

> Mary Lou 3, 8
> James 2, 3, 6, 8
> Tony 5, 7

The numbers refer to the skill areas to which you have assigned them.

Cover all of the material the children have mastered. You may be in for a surprise. You may find much of last year's math absolutely unknown. Don't blame the children. But whatever you find, you will have a blueprint for proceeding.

Discovering the child's inadequacies

You have your chart for quick reference but you also have a set of papers to review with each youngster. And you must start with him—with whatever skills he lacks—wherever he is.

Bunnie is a delightful little girl who is rather quiet, but smiling. In reviewing her work, which she sat over most diligently, her teacher found she could not subtract. Nor could she do anything more advanced. She had developed a block as far as math was concerned. Bunnie was in the eighth grade.

You may wish to have certain children work on problems with you. Do this on an individual basis. Have the youngster tell you, aloud, every step, as he works it out. In this way, you are able to spot the exact place where he goes wrong.

Review the paper and have the child show you the areas in

which he feels deficient. It is essential that he realize this deficiency and that he see the need for remedying it. "Why do I need this subject, anyway," they sometimes ask, and you may wish to answer "In your lifetime you may earn a quarter of a million dollars. Over a period of forty years, this is easily possible. Don't you need to know mathematics to take care of it? If you go to college, you will earn a half million—according to the U.S. Labor Department. Don't you have to know how to take care of it?"

You have your diagnostic list. What next? You may set up groups to work on the various areas. You would teach each group, and then have them work together. They can teach each other, do problems together, work as a unit. However, give homework to be done at home—alone. Check the progress of the group period- ically.

Some children need your individual assistance. For them, this help can be a matter of enabling them to progress. Where remediation is necessary because retardation is very severe, do the following:

Break down the topic to its very simplest aspect. Teach how this is done. Don't take it for granted that the child understands anything. Proceed step by step. When a child has developed a "mental block," try every device you can think of to remove the block. Cuissinaire rods, money, beans, an abacus, a flannel board, manipulative toys—whatever you can think of—to make the point.

Try to build an understanding. It is not enough, when you are dealing with a blocked child to say, "See, this is what you must do." He must see why the steps should be taken. Bunnie learned to subtract with pennies.

The actual situations were set up, and Bunnie was able to physically remove coins from stacks of ten. Then the stacks were lessened, and she had to borrow from next door neighbors. She enjoyed the game, but it took time for her to translate what she was doing to printed numbers. However, she did make progress, and did get past this mental stoppage.

Teaching the curriculum and the skill areas

You have another task to do—in addition to remediation. You have to teach the new work of the grade, as well. How can you do both effectively? One way is to divide the class time into two parts. One part is for skill training—and for remediation or enrichment. The second part is for covering the curriculum. You will have to play it by ear, to use your own judgment when it comes to the time allotments for each part. Study your checklist. If your youngsters need remediation badly—if more than 50 percent of them are behind—devote at least half of the time to group work or individual work in skills. You will have to prepare work for each group based exactly on its needs. Use the textbook or workbooks. Also, give homework in the skill. Have the children go over one another's work. Set up a cooperative situation. Check it yourself, too, from time to time. You must hammer away at this. You will be working with the groups, too. For those children who do not need skill teaching, we will suggest, further on, a great deal of work for them to do while this remediation is going on.

In regard to teaching the curriculum:

1. When you introduce a new topic try to keep the arithmetic aspect of it within the children's capabilities.

Let's say you are teaching the area of a rectangle. You know Sam has trouble with multiplication; but can grasp the concept of area. Give him problems he can handle. If he can see that a rectangle whose sides are 2" by 4" has an area of 8 square inches, he can learn the basic idea. Then, when he masters the multiplication table he will be able to work out other problems. Children often can understand concepts, but cannot do the problems because of their inability to work with numbers. When you grade their work, credit them with understanding the basis, even if the arithmetic is wrong. For your students who are retarded in math, this system can provide a tremendous ego boost because they are able to see that *they can learn.*

In working out problems in regard to area, have them write out each step, so that you can credit them.

Children who have developed problems with arithmetic need encouragement and reinforcement. The worst thing in the world is for the teacher to say, without any hostility, "Darling, what's the matter with you? Can't you see this?" The fault lies with the teacher, and previous teachers, not with the child.

In any dealing with children who are showing learning difficulties, move ahead as soon as they grasp something they've had difficulty with before. Don't linger any longer than is necessary. Make your groups fluid, and inform the children of this situation at the very beginning of the year. Keep them in motion, so that the children are kept on their toes, mentally.

If children seem resistant to some of your teaching, try to find other methods of covering the material on which you are working. Speak to other teachers, or to your supervisor. Check other textbooks. If you can, discuss the matter with college teachers. Look into the literature. Children, who cannot master skills, have serious problems. By trying to help them solve them, you are really doing vital teaching.

For the children who don't need remediation

What can you do with students who don't need remediation?

1. Give them additional practice in handling the area of the curriculum you are teaching. Make sure they understand it thoroughly, and can handle even difficult problems in the subject area. Textbooks supply the material for this.

2. Go deeper into the curriculum. Your class is working on the concept of area. Have them calculate the areas of the community you live, of the city, of the state. Of course these will not be accurate, but they can easily do approximations.

Prepare worksheets with depth problems which are of interest to them. How much of the earth's surface is land? How much is covered by water? How does the area a skyscraper takes up compare to its height? What area of the earth is occupied by each time zone? These are the type of questions they might work on.

3. Have them work on developing relationships between numbers. Call these "Puzzles" and give them the aura of fun.

Start by giving them several to figure out. Begin with simple ones, and then proceed to puzzles they are equipped to handle.

Ask them to supply the next two numbers to the series:

1,5,7,11,13,17,19,___,___
1,11,20,28,35,41,___,___
5,25,625, ___,___

These puzzles may involve fractions or decimals, positive or negative numbers—depending on the children's ability to handle them.

4. Once or twice a year, have the enrichment groups do research into "Occupations Involved with Arithmetic and Mathematics." Have them learn exactly what the work is, how the skill in math is used, how one prepares for this career in terms of educational training.

Such careers as accounting, bookkeeping, engineering, banking, architecture, and surveying might be considered.

5. Have the children do research in the arithmetical or mathematical aspect of:

> The Stock Market
> Our Monetary System
> Machine Shop Math
> Constructing a Building
> Surveying Land

6. Introduce topics which are advanced for them—such as elementary algebra.

7. Have them make graphs of class progress, their personal progress, temperature, barometric pressure.

8. Link math to science. Have them research the need for a knowledge of math in the sciences. How does a scientist use math in his work?

Above all, no useless busy work. Any project undertaken must be done well—and with understanding and care.

Combating carelessness, the big enemy

Children are careless. Adults are careless. But in this subject area it can be extremely detrimental. How can we combat it?

1. Teach your children to estimate so that they have an idea of about how much their answers should be. Then, when they differ considerably, the answers should be questioned. Make the estimating as simple as possible.

2. When you grade a test, you can say, at the top of the paper, 80 percent (would have been 92 percent except for careless errors). We have found this method quite successful. Point out

careless errors. No one wants to lose credit for anything as ridiculous as this type of error. Use this psychology with your children.

3. When you find a child is habitually careless, discuss it with him. Show how this type of sloppiness can be detrimental not only in arithmetic, but in other areas of living as well. If the child's appearance is such that you can truthfully say, "You don't dress carelessly. Why is your thinking careless?" don't reprimand him. Try instead, to teach him why the habit of being careful is worth developing.

4. Have the children review their work before submitting it. There is always the danger of making the same mistake again, but this can be diminished if the child does the example again on another sheet of paper. For particularly careless youngsters, this is almost a must.

5. Reward those children who carefully checked their own work and corrected their own errors. A five-point "bonus" can be an excellent incentive. Add it to the grade thusly:

> 80 plus 5 point bonus 85
> (In this way a child can score 105.)

Motivating children to check their papers carefully is very, very important.

Helping children to learn the steps in problem solving

As you work with individual children, try to get an idea of their thinking. This is particularly necessary in problem solving. If a child can solve the problems in a specific area, he doesn't need your individual attention, but if he cannot, sit down with him and have him tell you each step—in the order in which he takes them. You will find some youngsters who have no idea where to begin. Try to show them by questioning, rather than telling them the steps. Have them write the steps so that they can see them as well as hear them. You may wish to begin with,

1. "What are we trying to find out to solve this problem?" Continue with,

2. "What information are we given?"

3. Next, "How do we use this information?"

4. Then "What process must we use to solve this problem?"

You will find children who have no idea of how to determine what the problem is all about—or how to use the information given. Try to show them how to translate sentences into mathematical terms.

Consider the classic problem, "If you have $10, and you want to buy phonograph albums which cost $4.29, how many can you buy?" Show the child exactly how to use the questions listed above. "What are we trying to find out?" you ask. If the youngster doesn't answer correctly, rephrase the question this way, "What is this problem about?" This asks for a general answer. The child answers, "Phonograph records." "What about phonograph records?" you ask him. "They cost $4.29," he replies. "That's true," you respond. "But you're telling me a fact. What is the question this problem asks about the phonograph records?"

Discuss the problems. Take them apart. Show how each part of the problem as it is stated is important.

You may wish to have your capable students work with the less capable on this. This is worthwhile for both youngsters. It is very possible the bright child can approach his classmate on his own level.

Teaching the reading skills the child needs to succeed in arithmetic

Take nothing for granted! Make sure every child can read every word he needs to know in order to do his arithmetic. You will find many children "in the dark" in this regard. We have even seen youngsters use words—and then not recognize them when they had to read them.

Poor readers are often fazed by long words. They don't even try—they just assume they can't read them. Yet, if told what they are, they can follow through with the arithmetic. You may solve this problem in one of several ways:

1. The best—teach the vocabulary and consider the words as sight words which the child must learn.

2. Have all problems read aloud in class. Encourage the child to have someone help him at home with the reading of the problems.

3. Work with the child on an individual basis. Help him almost to memorize the vocabulary he needs. Encourage him to think he is able to function well in arithmetic—if he just gives himself a chance.

4. Encourage the child to use the techniques he was taught in reading class—such as phonetic analysis or structural analysis to figure out the words he encounters in math that he has not already learned.

The vocabulary of arithmetic

Teach the specific mathematical vocabulary you will be using. Teach it at the very beginning of the year, and then repeat the words once or twice a week to build a familiarity with them.

Miss G. was teaching one of the most mathematically-retarded classes in the school. Almost all of the children had had difficulty with arithmetic for years. She approached them, knowing this and taking it into consideration.

One day, she was discussing with the class the need for them to speak up if they didn't understand something.

"I realize you have problems in arithmetic," she said, "and I want to help you. I can't if you keep them from me. Suppose I said something about differential calculus."

"What's that?" one child asked.

"An advanced form of mathematics," Miss G. answered. "I knew you wouldn't know that. But what about mixed numbers?"

"I don't know what they are," another youngster said.

"Or decimals. Who doesn't know what decimals are?" This time there was half a dozen hands raised.

"What about dozen?" Two hands went up.

When this session was over, Miss G. had learned what it meant to be retarded in arithmetic, and where to begin her work. In vocabulary development, first.

Make as many concepts as you can clear to the children. For example, don't talk about circles or spheres. Show them. This is needed particularly by the retarded math students. However, many youngsters need help in going from the concrete to the abstract. If you're discussing temperature, show a thermometer. Don't assume the child has seen one. Use as many actual objects in your class as you can. They'll get a very good idea just how small 1/32 is—if you divide one pie among all of them!

Credit Official Photograph, Bd. of Ed., N.Y.C.

Figure 8-1

Helping the bright child to forge ahead

You may have a youngster in your class who is very bright in this area. What do you do to work with him?

1. Make sure he has mastered the areas you are teaching. Don't take it for granted that he has. Have him do work sheets which show he has completed these areas of learning.

2. Go into depth in the same areas. Develop work sheets with more thought-provoking problems. Relate your teaching to advanced concepts within the same realm.

3. If you are competent, introduce the child to advanced topics. For example, young children enjoy elementary algebra, and can make excellent progress in it. The bright child will often be able to move ahead in this area very rapidly, once he is headed in the right direction.

4. Have him teach other children. This gives him the experience of teaching. In fact, it may help him to find his vocation; and it will show him how to break ideas down into small units and build with those units.

5. Use the topics listed earlier in this chapter for enrichment.

6. If you do not feel competent in this area (and the vast, vast majority of teachers do not), consult with other teachers or with your supervisor. You may write to your State Education Department, usually located in the State Capital, requesting information and assistance. You may also consult the local college personnel.

7. Contact the child's parents. If they are willing to have you do so, and you are able to, teach the child checkers or chess. Both games involve the type of thinking very closely related to mathematics. The bright child may be very much benefited by this exposure—and he may be presented, in this way, with a lifetime hobby.

8. Ask the advanced student to develop games to be used in class based on arithmetic or mathematical concepts.

Games to make arithmetic fun

Think in terms of making this subject as much fun as possible. Instead of having worksheets all of the time, replace them with contests and an entirely different aspect will emerge. Drills are onerous, but when done under the guise of puzzles, they are different—and the children feel differently about them.

After you teach addition, request parental and supervisory permission—and teach the youngsters to play the card game "casino." They will get practice in adding, and while they are playing you have time for working with the children on an individualized basis. Dominoes may be used with the same result. Even "Scrabble" gives experiences in arithmetic.

Can you visualize the children's reactions? This isn't like an ordinary class. This is fun!

To give older boys and girls an exciting time, stage a contest based on any topic you are teaching. This should be done by teams. Divide the class; try to place one of the better students in each team. Give out worksheets, and tell the class, "Every example done correctly earns a point for your team." In this way even the less competent students are able to contribute.

Building objects to scale utilizes arithmetic skills, and teaches manual dexterity as well. A model city can be created with paper cubes. By making the "buildings" different sizes, the child becomes familiar with inches and parts of inches.

You may wish to have each child plan a budget for a party. This may be one he wishes to give, or one for the entire class. This is a meaningful way to teach budgeting. If you feel the children can afford it, have them chip in for the party. You'll all have fun.

Arithmetic baseball is another game we suggest. Have the children make up cards (5 x 7 index) with examples or problems on them. Number each card. Then have a key made up, either by the most advanced child, or by all the children. You are the only one to have the key. Have values attached to each card, in terms of 1 base, 2 bases, 3 bases or Home Run. Of course these would be related to the difficulty of the example:

```
#42
3 1/2 x 9 2/3 =
3 bases
```

You should have about 150 of these cards. If each child makes 5 or 6, you will have a sufficient number. Have two teams. Each team has as many members as necessary to place every child in the class.

When a child goes up to bat, he gets his card, and writes the problem on the board. He then works it out—while the opposing team does. If he is wrong they have to get him out—by showing his answer is incorrect.

The game is then played like baseball. When a team gets three outs the opposing side comes to bat. After nine innings, the side with the most runs wins.

This may be done with very simple arithmetic in the lower grades, or more complex math in the upper. It is good practice, and can be made very exciting.

The arithmetic laboratory

Toward the end of the year, if you wish to, you may set up an arithmetic laboratory. Point out that in laboratories scientists solve problems. Construct a series of problems for each child to solve. Base these on the areas with which he has had difficulty. Allow the children to seek help in solving their problems. Tell them they may consult their textbooks, their notebooks, their classmates, their friends, you. The objective is to solve these problems—and to learn how to solve similar problems in the future. Give them a time limit, and make sure they understand they cannot waste even precious minutes.

Encourage them to try different solutions, to use diagrams and to write up their work as clearly as possible.

At the end of the year, use the textbook to make up another series of diagnostic tests. Include the curriculum of this year, and that of previous years.

You should see a decided improvement, but don't expect every child to know every topic perfectly.

You can give out worksheets for over-the-summer vacation if you wish, in order to prevent the child from losing some of the progress he has made. Say to the children, "This is good rainy day work. Don't do it if you can be outside playing. But, if the weather is bad, you can do yourself a lot of good by working on this." Over the summer, some children lose much of what they have learned before. Others lose less, but there is usually some loss. You can prevent this and, incidentally, endear yourself to the parents by presenting the children with summer work.

9

Developing more meaningful experiences in social studies through individualization

Years ago, certain subjects were referred to as history, geography, current events. Today we link them together in one large area we call social studies. There is another major difference—or there should be. Social studies are involved with people. Geography is studied in terms of the people who live in the different areas of the world, and their needs and problems. History is taught through the lives of individuals as well as nations. Current events deals with what is happening to people today—the history of tomorrow.

But social studies must involve much more. It must be a living course—teaching our children skills in living. They must learn how to work with others, how to get along, how to negotiate, and how to compromise. It must teach them how to understand the other guy and the problems he faces. For ours is a world filled with problems—with people going to bed hungry, or not even having a bed—and sleeping as they do in India, on the streets. Many of our children are far more fortunate than others, but we must teach all of them to feel for others as well as themselves.

In social studies, then, it is incumbent upon us to teach many, many aspects of the subject. We must teach our children to read maps, but also to think about the people living in the cities which they see as mere dots. We must teach them facts, but also how to interpret these facts in terms of human beings and their needs. We may teach them about methods of farming, but always with the idea in mind that, if these methods need improvement, someone must help the farmer to improve them.

Individualizing instruction is necessary if we are to help each child to learn the skills he personally needs to survive and to be a happy human being. The child must learn cooperation, since, if he is like most of us, he will be working and dealing with people during most of his adult life. He must learn to give and to take. Neither behavior, alone, will bring happiness. He must learn to look at others, feel for them, and if he possibly can, help them. He must learn to take his place in society, to contribute to it, and to take an active part in it.

Our news media fill the air constantly. Yet their reports need interpretation. Our youngsters must be able to actually do the

Credit Official Photograph, Bd. of Ed., N.Y.C.

Figure 9-1

interpreting. Other reading material, including textbooks, requires interpretation, as well.

Determining the child's ability to handle social studies skills

Much of your diagnosis, in this situation, is dependent upon your own observations. Some of it will be in regard to factual material and concepts, as well. Once again, we suggest a checklist. Here are some of the items you may wish to include. You will, of course, vary this according to the grade level. However, even second graders can be considered in terms of their relationships with the rest of the girls and boys.

After the class has been in progress for a month, you should be able to answer some, if not all, of these questions. They will give you the basis for individualizing your instruction. You have a curriculum to cover, of course, but you can easily do so and still teach the skills outlined here. For example, your class is studying Mexico. Establish committees. Ask the committee to elect a chairman. Give the committee a broad assignment, and access to as many resources as possible. Then select a topic which is very broad and encompassing. How does the average Mexican person, who lives in the country, live? How does he live, if he is a city dweller? What is his whole life like? What does he do to earn his living? What kind of house does he live in? What kind of food does he eat? What kind of medical care does he receive? What is his education? Give as much information as you can, with ideas such as these in mind.

Here are some of the social skills you will be looking at:

1. Does the child consider the welfare of others as well as his own?

2. Is he open minded to other children's ideas?

3. Is he willing to discuss them?

4. Can he express himself well in a discussion group?

5. Is he sympathetic to the needs of others?

6. Is he able to communicate his ideas to other children? To adults?

These are the academic skills:

1. Does he learn the facts necessary for this grade?

2. Is he able to comprehend the concepts you are teaching to him?

Willowbrook to get donations for rides

By ROBERT MIRALDI

"I didn't even know what a glider was until I saw the picture in the paper," Donna LaManna, 10, a sixth-grader at P r a l l Intermediate School, mused. "I don't know any kids at Willowbrook, but I know they need help."

Not many, if any, of the youngsters at the West Brighton school knew too much a few weeks ago about the Glider Fund set up to buy recreational rides for Willowbrook State School.

But once they found out they put down their heads and plunged full-speed ahead into a fund-raising drive that so far netted $420 and is still rolling.

"It's just tremendous," Guy V. Molinari, the fund's organizer, said. "I hope some of the other schools will get involved and perhaps do as much."

Molinari had more reason to be happy than just the Prall contribution to the fund, since his own efforts are paying dividends, too. The fund so far has a massed $1,700, thanks to 104 individual contributions.

The first unit has been ordered and, according to Molinari, it won't be long, perhaps next week. before the first ride will be installed on Willowbrook grounds.

The Prall effort, to climax Friday with a flea market sale. took shape two weeks ago when school teachers mentioned the fund to various students.

OTHERS JOINED

"It started out as a sixth-grade project," Mrs. Muriel Karlin, assistant principal, said "But all the students — the seventh and eighth grades — became interested, too. The whole project has created a social consciousness in the school. It's teaching the children to care about people."

The students reached the $420 mark with a cake sale, a newspaper drive and individual collection. Sixth-graders Elisa Brahn and Barbara Riegler collected over $100 between them.

Kenny Bethel, 13, got the ball rolling in the eighth grade.

"The teachers mentioned what it was for, so we started to raise money. My grandfather used to work there, and I saw a lot of the kids... That's how I knew about it."

Along with the Prall contribution, Molinari has received substantial gifts from the Nassau Smelting and Refining Co., Tottenville, and the North Shore Post, Veterans of Foreign Wars, Westerleigh.

David Eisenstein, a 10-year old sixth-grader, said that "almost everybody gave when they heard what it was for."

Contributions are being sent to the Glider Fund at 88 New Dorp Plaza. Checks should be made payable to First National City Bank.

Credit Staten Island Advance, Oct. 11, 1972.

Figure 9-2

3. Is he able to read maps? Latitude, longitude, comparative positions of nations?

4. Is he able to use the information he has learned to prove a point in a discussion?

5. Does he accept everything he reads, or does he question?

6. Will he look at both sides before he decides on an issue?

7. Is he able to use a variety of resource materials?

We suggested an assignment, above. If it is assigned to a committee, the youngsters are placed in a situation where they should be working together. You can assess the leadership quality, too. You can see if the children can interpret facts—and you can develop an understanding of, and a feeling for, people of another culture.

Handling the curriculum

You have an extensive curriculum to cover in social studies. However, it can be taught at the same time that you present experiences to the children which will help them to develop attitudes they need if they are to be successful human beings living in our society. The secret is in your planning. Begin at the very start of the term—and work out the year's material. Decide on priorities. What are the concepts you feel the children must learn? What are the factual areas? Then structure the social experiences the children will have. You will have to decide, then, which areas can best be covered by discussion. Next, which can be best handled by committee work. Then, which will be most suited by research reporting; which by panel discussions. Work this out in advance, and you will find that your time is best used in this way. Plan trips which fit the curriculum. Every time you take a trip you have the opportunity to get closer to your children, and even to do individual instruction in an informal setting. Plan, too, those times when you will be using audio-visual aids.

As you come to the end of the seventh month of the school year, give the children a listing of the specific information for which you will be holding them responsible. Include facts, concepts, theories. Tell them that if they learn all of the information included, they can score 100 percent. (This is too simple, you are thinking. It isn't. In spite of this, many children will still not master the material. If they do, they deserve the 100 percent. But they will learn far more this way—by having very specific material, than they would studying "in the dark.")

Don't feel you are bound to the curriculum. You have it within your power to teach it—and, at the same time, to give your children experiences to prepare them for life.

Reading in the social studies area

Reading is, of course, essential to the area of social studies, and every child needs certain reading skills if he is to be successful in this, or any other, academic field. Certain skills are particularly relevant. You can teach a reading skill at the same time you are covering the curriculum. In fact, you will find the children are reading with far more concentration if you ask them to "find the main idea and related details to substantiate it." Reading skills are just that—devices to help the child to read more skillfully. As you assign a particular topic, add a reading skill as well, and observe the result.

In the area of comprehension, children should be able to:

1. Find the main idea and related details to substantiate it.
2. Organize and classified facts.
3. Perceive a sequence of ideas.
4. Draw inferences and conclusions.
5. Understand problems.
6. Form judgments.
7. Read critically—distinguishing fact from opinion.
8. Understand relationships.

In the area of work-study skills, the youngsters should be able to:

1. Understand the index of a text.
2. Use the dictionary.
3. Use the encyclopedia.
4. Use the atlas.
5. Use the almanac.
6. Interpret maps.
7. Interpret graphs.
8. Adjust their reading rates to material being read:

   a. Skim for finding information.
   b. Careful reading for digesting information.
9. Select and evaluate information.

Select those skills which are applicable to your grade level. Help each child develop them. For enrichment, have the advanced youngsters work on new, more sophisticated skills. By junior high all of the youngsters should have had some training in all of these skill areas.

After you have taught or reviewed this material, prepare a rexographed sheet for each of these skill areas. Have the children work on these. As you grade them, you can determine which child needs more practice in any given area.

You may find it a better procedure to have the youngsters work on different skills, so that the resources are not overtaxed.

Another method of determining which skills should be retaught is by use of the contract. (See Chapter 10). As you review the child's work with him, you will be able to tell by observation which skills he lacks.

Teaching the vocabulary of social studies

1. In using social studies texts or resource materials, your children will encounter words with which they are unfamiliar. (If they do not, the material you are covering is too simple for them.) The dictionary is the best source for finding the meaning of a new word as it is used in the sentence. Many words have multiple meanings. The children must learn to use the key words in the sentence or paragraph to help them choose the meaning which is most suitable.

To teach this, you will need several paragraphs containing words with multiple meanings. Duplicate these paragraphs, underlining the problem words. Have the children look up the words in their dictionaries, and copy the various meanings. Then discuss the key words in each paragraph which help them to choose the correct meaning.

To reinforce this, have the children use the words in sentences that explain their meaning.

2. Consider words which are commonly used but may have a special meaning in regard to social studies. "Age" is one. We say

this is the "age of steel"; yet children associate age with a number of years. "Strike" means one thing to a baseball enthusiast, another to a worker. Clarify any such meanings.

One class was discussing burial places.

"When someone dies, what do they do with the head?" one child asked.

"What do you mean?" the teacher looked perplexed.

The child repeated, "When someone dies, what do they do with the head?"

"They bury it," the teacher replied.

"Are you sure?" the child asked. Then she added, "I know they bury the body. But do they bury the head?"

3. Have the children keep vocabulary lists of their own. Have them list the words they have just learned, with their meanings. Encourage them to review these words—and once a month collect the lists and have a vocabulary bee—similar to the spelling bees of old.

4. A fine way to learn the meaning of a new word is to have the children compose or find an interesting sentence containing it, and memorize the sentence.

For example, to emphasize the meaning of the word "preempt"—"My kitten always preempts the most comfortable chair in the living room."

5. A teacher should never be reluctant to use her full vocabulary when speaking to the children. She will find, at the end of the term, that much of it has been absorbed by the youngsters. To her delight, they will be using many of her words and expressions. Even if the children do not fully understand the meaning of the word, it is no longer a complete stranger to them. The children really are interested in new words and benefit from exposure to them.

We can never over-emphasize vocabulary development. It is the basis for communication, and is also one of the ways in which intelligence is measured.

Debates and panel discussions, and helping each child prepare for them

As stated before, our children must learn to present their thoughts clearly and succinctly. To teach them to do this, debates and panel discussions are particularly good.

Plan to give each child a chance to participate in one of these activities at least once a month. About a week to ten days before, assign a topic. Have the children who are participating research it, and list the points they plan to make. Three or four days before the event, review the points with them. Make sure they have enough information, understand it, and can present it well. If necessary, work on their speech and their delivery with them. Encourage audience participation in the form of questioning and comments. Open the floor to the rest of the class when the presentation is over. Have the youngsters who did the presentation write their information on the board, so that the work they did permanently benefits the other children.

Debates and discussions of this type are very valuable in giving children self-confidence and in teaching them to present their ideas. The debate should be on a subject where there is some controversy. The panel discussion may be on any topic you care to present. Inform the children at the start of the year that they will all be called upon for these programs. So often, only the most verbal children will be asked to do this type of work. The ones who need it most are allowed to sit back or to hide. It is your shy child, your reticent youngster, who will derive the most from this experience.

There are added benefits. Should you be called upon to present an assembly program, you can have a debate or panel discussion. Your children are already familiar with the procedures—and have already spoken before a group. You can even repeat a debate or discussion you had in class, providing it was a stimulating one. Furthermore, for Open School Week, or whenever parents visit your class while it is in session, these activities are very fine. You will want every child to take part. You can bring them in by asking each boy or girl to ask one question relevant to the program which has just been presented.

Individualizing instruction in regard to social attitudes

Most of us realize today how cruel and unfashionable it is to be a bigot. One of the most popular television programs points out how ridiculous a prejudiced person often appears. Yet, there are still bigoted parents who affect their children. Have you seen a boy or girl, not yet in the teens, who says, "I can't stand_____

————," naming a group of people. Have you heard jokes which denigrate whole nationalities?

If you find you have in your class children who reveal these attitudes, it is extremely important that you work with them. First, the topic must be brought out—after an incident, if one occurs. If not, whenever it is relevant. But a discussion between you and the child must take place. You may begin by asking the youngster if he has ever heard the Indian proverb, "Do not judge another until you have walked in his moccasins for one month." Then proceed with this idea of changing places. "Would you like to be in Jack's shoes?" you ask. "Why not?" Try to find out why the child feels the way he does, and to attack the problem at the root. This is a long, time-consuming subject, but a very important one. Don't feel you are being wasteful if you spend precious minutes or hours on it. If you are taking your class on a trip, this is an excellent time for this kind of discussion, since you can develop a rapport with the child under the informal trip conditions.

If there are members of others groups in your class, arrange for the bigoted child to work on committees with them. This is one of the best ways to break down prejudice. Team membership, too, is very good. If you can give children shared interests they often become good friends.

Other attitudes, such as getting along with other people, working well with them, and making compromises when they are necessary, should be brought up for class discussion. One of the best techniques for this is "buzz sessions." Group the children in groups of 5 or 6, give them a problem to solve, and have them work at it for a limited period of time. (15 to 20 minutes is about right.) Have a leader established within each group. He will be the one to report the group's findings back to the entire class. Use topics worded in this way:

1. "John is assigned to your committee. A chairman is elected, and topics decided upon for each person. John accepts his, but then does not do it. What can the committee do? What should the leader do?"

2. "Your class is being disciplined because three boys destroyed another boy's work. What can you do about it?"

3. "Your teacher asked the members of the class if they would like to go on a trip. Everyone agreed. But when it came to

deciding where to go, the children could not agree. Finally three places emerged. How should this matter be settled?"

4. "Someone in the class steals pens. No one knows who. Then it is discovered the guilty person is a very quiet little girl. What should be done about her?"

5. "One child never has lunch. His family cannot afford to give him money for it. What can be done about this?"

Bringing the child and television together intelligently

It is a rare child indeed who is not subjected to the mass media. Television is, of course, the prime example. Statistics prove to us that the amount of time the average child spends in front of the set rivals closely the number of hours he spends in school. Television can be a tremendous teacher. We have seen two-year-olds count to 15 because they learned to do so from watching "Sesame Street." Older children, and adults, too, can learn from it—if their viewing is guided. It is not too difficult a task for you to do this guiding. Let us suggest how:

1. You may write to the major stations asking for advance announcements. These are often available for a full month in advance; or you may consult the Sunday newspapers, or *TV Guide* for the programs of the week ahead.

2. Review the listing and select programs for your entire class, and for specific children. The child who is interested in music will enjoy programs which might bore the others. The same is true of other programs.

3. Give specific assignments. Even the 5W's (who, what, when, where, why,) can suffice. (Who or what was the program about? When did it take place? Where? Why was it produced? Why did you watch it? What did you learn?)

4. For teaching current events, there really can be no substitute for television. However, we would suggest you emphasize programs such as documentaries. But avoid newscasts or documentaries if they show much bloodshed or violence. The television studios seem to have no restrictions when it comes to these aspects. Indeed, the news is often bloody, but our children do not have to watch this. For the sensitive youngster, it may be very upsetting. However, documentaries on such subjects as poverty or drug abuse may open the child's eyes to the problems some of our people face—far more graphically than reading about it.

Teaching children critical thinking

Every child should learn to think critically. This is really a very tall order, because even the most sophisticated person is sometimes taken in by words which are expressly designed for that purpose.

Give all of your children the basis for critical thinking. A sample dialogue follows.

> "Who can tell us how many people live in India?" you ask.
> One child volunteers, "A lot." she says.
> "But how many?" you pursue.
> "A million," another suggests.
> "How many people live in our country?"
> "Two hundred million," another child answers.
> "Are you sure?" you ask.
> "Yes" the child replies.
> "That's approximate—but close. Then could there be a million in India?" you again question.
> "No, there would have to be more," one child answers.
> Another volunteers, "Are there a billion?"
> "What do you think boys and girls?" you ask. "Are there a billion?"
> The class discusses this among themselves.
> "Let's take a vote," you suggest. "How many think there are a billion?"
> About ten raise their hands.
> "A million?" About fifteen raise their hands.
> "Who wins?" you ask.
> "I guess its a million," a child responds. "But I don't believe it."
> "Why?"
> "Because I know there are more than that."
> "But the class voted on it," you reply.
> "So what," Tim answers. "How can people vote on a fact?"
> "What do you suggest?" you ask the class.
> "Let's look it up."

Can you see how this is an exercise in critical thinking? Many children get the idea that voting on something decides it. What could be further from the truth?

When your youngsters make statements in social studies particularly, have them back them up with facts. In practice "Let's look it up" should be a slogan.

If you find a child who seems to be very unsophisticated and gullible, work with him. Call each incident where he is "taken in" to his attention. Children may dupe others—a not unusual occurrence. If this happens treat it lightly, but privately, explain what is happening so the youngster becomes aware of it.

Teaching children how to read news reports in both newspapers and magazines . . . with a grain of salt!

Have your children bring in various reports of the same stories. The variation can be amazing. Try to get the earliest reports, and then later ones. Have the children make comparisons. Haven't you seen figures change drastically as facts emerge?

However, every child should be made aware of how to read newspaper stories. The first two paragraphs, as a rule, are very short summaries of what is to come.

You may wish to have a short review of the news as part of every day's work. This can be done by having one child review the newspaper the night before, select three stories and report on them to the class. You can, if you feel it is necessary, go over the report before it is given. This might be a good idea while you are establishing the routine. It shouldn't be necessary for the entire year.

Have them compare stories in the papers with those which appear in the news magazines later on. This, too, is work in critical thinking. Are there differences? If so, why?

Another interesting exercise is to have your children compare the written reports with those given on radio and television.

Ask the children to volunteer for this work. Have them listen to radio, or watch television news programs and take notes. These are then compared with the stories which appear in the press. Again, they will discover discrepancies. Use them as the basis for discussion and for developing critical thinking. Try this with weather reports, too.

Committee work to teach the children how to work with others

Because committee work helps to develop a great many of the skills we are stressing in social studies, we are going to discuss it in greater detail.

Your committees should be flexible. Set them up, and when they have completed their work, dissolve them and establish new ones.

Give each committee a definite assignment. Have the group elect a chairman. (It is up to you to make sure the same children are not elected repeatedly.) Then have the children divide up the work among themselves.

Credit Official Photograph, Bd. of Ed., N.Y.C.

Figure 9-3

Expect a certain amount of noise, as the work progresses.

Have the children determine, for themselves, which resources they will use—encyclopedias, books, maps, filmstrips, or atlases. Have as many available as you can.

Review, with the children, the form their reporting will take. If possible, allow them to select it. It need not always be the same. One time, they may have a panel discussion. Another time, they may write a plan incorporating the research they have done. They may construct a newspaper—an excellent device, but one requiring a good deal of time.

Your role in this is to act as a guide, an advisor. It is also to work with individual children, assisting them in problem solving, or in any area in which you feel they need help. You may find yourself working on reading skills, which Johnny needs, while the rest of the class is involved with one project or another.

Once in a while, you may have the children do dioramas. Another time they may draw scenes. But these activities do not

Credit Official Photograph, Bd. of Ed., N.Y.C.

Figure 9-4

teach too much, so that an overexpenditure of time on them should be avoided.

Have each committee report, when its work is completed. This may be done by one child, or by all, depending on the topic.

Use your committees to give your youngsters experiences in working together, and to give you the opportunity to work with individual children.

Trips

No social studies program can be successful without taking the youngsters on a number of trips. They need to be exposed to the outside world—outside the classroom.

A trip need not be a monumental task. Divide the class into groups, and have each select a leader, or you may choose the leader if you wish. Then, instead of counting heads constantly, you have the leader report to you after he has counted the children in his group. This simple procedure can make your day infinitely easier.

We have seen trips used as motivation, and prove extremely effective, even with the most disruptive children.

Choose places which tie in with your curriculum—in either science or social studies. You would be amazed at the number of children who have never seen an airport—even though there may be one relatively close by. Or a building site. Or a local wholesale fruit or vegetable distributor. Or a municipal market. Try to think of the places your community and neighboring communities have to offer.

Again, let us say that during your trips you have an opportunity for very valuable individualized instruction. The informal setting of a bus is great for communicating, and for teaching. Not teaching reading, of course, but teaching social attitudes, for example.

Mrs. H. was a new teacher, the sixth the class had had in five months. As she entered the class, one boy shouted, "When are you leaving? You ain't gonna stay. No teacher can take us for more than a couple of days."

Mrs. H. not only stayed, but she had the children under control, and working (albeit they did have many problems). She did it by taking 24 trips in the five months she taught the class. She discovered many of the children had never been out of their immediate neighborhood. "Juan," she said, "had never been on a New York subway—although he was born and brought up in the Bronx. Clarice had never seen an elephant, although she lived within two miles of an excellent zoo. I found I had to give these underprivileged children the experiences most middle class parents give to their children when they are very young. Betty, aged 14, insisted on a pony ride. Betty needed that ride. I really learned that term what it meant to be disadvantaged. So many of us take things like trips to the zoo for granted. But all children do not get them."

If you have children who lack such fundamentals, try to fill them in. For your more fortunate children, there are still a plethora of "adventures" for them—because that is what the boys and girls really consider trips—adventures. We learned that from a little girl, her eyes open like saucers, who said "This is a real adventure," as she rode up a high-speed elevator.

Summary

In social studies, we are not concerned primarily with subject matter. We should place our emphasis on the development of the child in terms of his behavior with other human beings. Although there is a curriculum to cover, it can be done very effectively while, at the same time, we are giving each child the opportunity to work with others. Committee work is excellent for this. We are also anxious to find the child's needs, of a social nature, and help him to satisfy them. Much of our diagnosis will be by observation, and by listening carefully to what the children tell us.

We should work, too, to help each child to learn those work-study skills which he will need as he furthers his education. We can take these into consideration as we cover the curriculum areas designated for the particular grade. Since reading is a particularly important tool in this area, it is worth considering in terms of specific goals. We must work on vocabulary development, as well.

Interaction with other human beings requires communication, and one of our goals should be to help each child become more verbal, and express himself more clearly and intelligently. We suggest panel discussions and debates for this purpose.

Individualized instruction is particularly necessary for the child who is bigoted. You have an obligation to work with such a child to overcome this handicap.

In social studies, too, we try to teach our children to think critically, especially in regard to the mass media. Television, the newspapers and the magazines should be read with a careful eye.

Our children are often taught by a teacher lecturing, rather than by the teacher structuring the class so the children will have valuable experiences. The latter is extremely essential, and it is with this in mind that we suggest committee work and trips as being almost essential to the effective teaching of social studies.

10

How individualized instruction can improve your science teaching

If you have seen pre-school children, we are sure you have noticed their almost insatiable curiosity. They are, almost constantly, asking, "Why" this or "Why" that. The world around them is filled with wonder and excitement. But, so often, by the time the child has reached the second or third grade, this has disappeared. Now it is our turn to ask why. There are, in education today, trends toward replacing this interest and this involvement. Open-corridor classes are one technique which is being attempted. However, even without this type of structured class, you can restore your pupils' intellectual curiosity—through an individualized approach to the science program.

Science is far more than a vast body of facts. Of course, it is an approach to facts as well, but it is a basic questioning. It is really the study of a whole world of "whys" and "hows." "Why is the sky blue? How deep is the ocean? Why is the grass green? How high is the sky?" As we become more scientifically sophisticated, the questions become more difficult. Why do sunspots affect our weather? How do radio waves carry across the earth? Why do bacteria produce illness? How can we use the huge oceans of the earth to produce food? But it is always a questioning, a desire to understand the world around us.

So, too, it should be—in our teaching. We have to re-instill in our little ones that scientific curiosity they once had—not so long ago.

How can you do this? You place a bottle with an uninflated balloon over its neck in a place which is warmed by the sun. To insure safety, obtain the bottle from a store that sells scientific equipment. As the air in the bottle expands, it fills the balloon—it "blows it up." You haven't said a word to the children. Someone asks,

"Who blew up the balloon?"

What do you answer? Would you believe that, in this moment, you can make or break a child's interest in science? You can say "That's a good question; look up the answer for homework." How do you think the child would react? Or you could answer with another question.

"What's all around us?" you ask. Johnny promptly volunteers, "Kids." Everyone laughs. "Good," you say. "Johnny you're very observant."

"What else is there all around us?" Now every hand is up.

"The walls," one child says.

"Excellent. What else?"

"The ceiling," another quickly volunteers.

"Fine. What else?"

"The desks," still another little one adds.

"Very good," you comment. "Anything else? Anything which might be in that bottle?"

Someone asks, very questioningly, "Air?"

"Where," you ask, "where is air? I don't see it. Do you see it? Who thinks there is air in the room?"

Some hands go up. "Anyone tell us about air?," you ask.

"You can't see it," a little girl announces.

"Then how do we know it's there? What would happen to you if there were no air?"

"You'd die."

"You certainly would. Who saw pictures of the astronauts on the moon? What do they carry on their backs?"

At this point, you produce a photograph of this scene—with the tanks clearly visible. Then you ask, "Who's seen pictures of underwater divers? What do they need in order to remain alive?"

Next you ask, "Why don't we need tanks of air?"

From here you go on to talk about what happens when anything is heated. It's not necessary to give a long, involved explanation—simply that when things are heated they get bigger. This happens to air, too.

"How many of you have ever been sick?"

The hands go up.

"Have had a fever?"

More hands are raised.

"What does your mother do to find out exactly how much fever?"

"She takes my temperature."

"Good! What does she use?"

They'll know the word thermometer. Not each child, but most of them.

"And, if your sick, your temperature will have gone up. There's a chemical in that thermometer. It's silver colored—anyone know what it is?" Someone may know the word.

You may produce a thermometer, and pass it around.

"What did we say happened when something is heated?"

"It gets bigger."

"Fine. Now if this thermometer is heated, where could this silver stuff—it's called mercury—where could it go?"

"It could move up."

Now, you ask the children to rub their hands together, hard. What happens? (They get quite warm.)

Then *you* rub your hands, with the thermometer between them. (There is danger of breaking it—so you do it.)

(Or you may put the thermometer in warm water. But this often results in broken thermometers, unless the temperature of the water is from 96-100 F.)

"Let's get back to the air," you say. Now, you question,

"What has this to do with answering our question? Who blew up the balloon?"

"No one," they answer.

"No one," you look incredulous! "Then what happened? Can anyone tell me what happened?"

"The air got bigger and filled it up."

"Wonderful," you reply. "Could you do this little experiment at home—what would you need?"

And so forth. The children are involved in this lesson because they are *thinking. You* have been able to direct *their thinking by your questions.* You've introduced new material. You've taught them many facts. But most of all, they have figured out why—why that balloon got bigger. And in the figuring, their curiosity is kept alive.

For the children who are interested, you may introduce simple experiments they can do at home, either in regard to expansion or air. Request the youngsters to prepare their experiments so they can do them for the entire class. (Help them, of course.) It is essential that they explain the results they obtained and why they got them.

Experiments for each child

Science is almost synonymous in a child's mind with experiments. They become particularly valuable when *the child* performs them. Here are some points to keep in mind.

1. An experiment can be very simple—but it should answer a question.

   a. What happens if we place a white cloth on our window sill and leave it there for two days?

   b. What happens if we do not give a plant water?

2. After the child reaches a conclusion, have him explain the result. This would, of course, be explained on his own level, but he should draw the conclusion himself.

For question "a" above, a second grader might say the cloth got dirty. A fifth grader might describe the different particles present on the cloth.

Both, however, can reach the conclusion that this dirt comes from the air. It may be particles of soil or pollutants.

3. Teach children to use a control whenever they perform an experiment.

A control is as simple as keeping a piece of cloth the same size on a closed window sill, or using two plants the same size, one of which is not watered, whereas the other receives normal care.

4. Encourage the children to keep a science notebook, and write

Credit Official Photograph, Bd. of Ed., N.Y.C.

Figure 10-1

up every experiment they do. Some will do many more than others. A simple account:

Problem
Method
Observation
Conclusion

will suffice. If a child wishes to embellish this with diagrams, of course you will encourage him to do so.

5. When a child shows he is interested, give him additional work to do.

Develop a repertoire of experiments. You may keep them on index cards. All you need to indicate is the problem and the method.

You will find such experiments in textbooks, lab manuals, teachers' guides. The children, too, will come up with excellent ones. For example, one second grader came in saying,

"I saw these paper towels advertised on TV. The lady said they picked up more water than other towels. So I decided to try it. They really do. I saw it myself."

6. Encourage the children to develop their own experiments. These are usually as good as those which come from books, and sometimes better.

"I heard you could make yogurt at home," one sophisticated young lady said. "I decided to see if I could. It's easy—and it's good, too."

Learning to test something out is really learning science.

7. Your children will love to work with chemicals. Chemical changes particularly attract them. However, be sure they do not handle poisons or inflammable materials. Give very specific quantities and instructions, and supervise them.

8. Decide on safety rules before any child does even one single experiment. Caution the youngster to check with you if he is uncertain about any procedure.

9. The children often need just a bit of help from you. Do you recall James Thurber's great story—of the time he had to do a drawing of something on a slide under a microscope? By careful focusing, he very clearly saw and drew his own eye.

10. Have each child do experiments concerning his own person, and his reactions. Teach him to take his pulse, and then, if he is healthy (and his doctor has no objections), have him run in place for one minute and take it again. Have him feel his heartbeat. If you are using the microscope, have him look at the cells from his own cheek, or his own hair follicles.

You may wish to have him check his weight against normal weight tables. If you do this, be prepared to help him to learn about proper nutrition, so that, perhaps, he can bring his weight up or down, if need be.

You may wish to have him measure the length of time he can hold his breath. The longer he can, the greater a vital capacity he has. (This, too, should be done only with a doctor's permission. A child with a heart ailment might become ill as a result. Of course, we would not want this to happen.)

The scientific method

Some sage once said, "There is nothing so difficult as the real labor of thinking." Without question, this is true. Thinking is hard work—thinking a problem through even more so. One of our tasks in the teaching of science is to teach our children to solve problems by thinking systematically and carefully. Scientists use the so-called scientific method, which can be applied to most problems—of any nature, scientific or otherwise.

Briefly the scientific method consists of:

1. Clearly stating the problem.

2. Getting as much information as necessary.

3. Using this information to figure out a solution to the problem. This is called a hypothesis.

4. Testing the hypothesis to determine whether or not it works.

5. If it does, the problem is solved. If not, figure out another possible hypothesis and test that.

6. Continue until a solution which is workable is found.

How can a child use this method of reasoning? Billy wants to use his bike. He finds it has a flat. His problem is "How to fix the flat." He examines the tire carefully.

"I don't see any cuts or nails or anything." He takes the bicycle to a gas station, puts air into it. Then, as he rides home, he feels the tire going flat again.

"What else could be wrong?" He examines the bike again. This time he finds a place where the tire is off the wheel. He pushes it into place, returns for more air, and drives off. Again it goes flat.

"Now, why is this happening?" Billy decides to go to the bicycle shop. He tells the shopkeeper his problem. This gentleman examines the tire. "No wonder you couldn't find it," he said. "There's a defective valve, and the air is escaping through it." When the valve was fixed, the tire kept its air.

Billy probably wasn't even aware of using the scientific method—but he was.

As you teach your children how to reason scientifically, you may point out the fact that Thomas A. Edison tried more than a thousand filaments before he found a suitable one for the electric light bulb.

The scientific method is used constantly as scientists develop one hypothesis, try it out, find it doesn't work, develop another, try it out—and so on and so forth.

Ask your youngsters to give you examples of how they might use this scientific method. Have each one "set up" a problem. They do not have to perform the actual experiment, but have them show how they would gather information, make hypotheses and test them out. When they can do the actual problem solving—so much the better.

You will find some children who cannot get past that initial hypothesis. (Even adults will sometimes become blocked—and almost stop functioning.) Work with them, showing them there are usually many possible answers. The point is to find the most workable solution.

Individualizing the curriculum

As in every subject area, you have a curriculum to cover. This needs variation to suit the needs of the individual child. One method of doing this is by the preparation of contracts. A contract is a series of questions and problems which the child must solve by finding the answers for himself. He may use any one of a number of resources—from textbooks to reference books to filmstrips or recordings. Of course, you do not have to prepare a different contract for each child. Group your children, and prepare a contract for each group. Perhaps you would require five different contracts for the entire class, ranging in complexity from contracts for the comparatively slower pupils to the very bright.

One big advantage of using a contract is that the child seeks to find information on his own. He is forced to think. He cannot sit by, just listening, as the lesson proceeds around him. He learns, too, to use other sources of information besides his ears. He is actively participating. He may not remember everything he looks up, but he will probably recall more than if he heard it in class. Another advantage is that the work is geared to the child's ability, and so he is not defeated before he starts. Furthermore, while the children are working on their contracts, you are able to do individualized instruction.

The contract which follows was prepared by Mrs. Roberta Schoenbrun, of the Oceanside School District, Oceanside, N.Y., for use with a 4th-grade class. It will give you an idea of the format of the contract.

Name   Date
Grade 4   Science, Unit VI

CONTRACT FOR MATTER AND ENERGY

A. Matter
   I. Read "Material of the Earth," pages 99-105; on a separate sheet of paper write your answers to the following in complete sentences:
       1. What is the definition of matter?
       2. What are the 3 different states of matter?
       3. Describe each state of matter and tell how each is different from the other.
       4. Draw a picture or cut one from a magazine to show each form of matter.
       5. Is air matter? Remember the definition of matter! To prove your answer, plan a demonstration.
       6. Make a list of 12 things in the room and write which state of matter each belongs in.
       7. Can matter change from one state to another? Give 3 examples. Plan a demonstration for the class.
       8. Make up a quiz of 5 questions for the other groups. Be sure to write the answers to the questions.

Name   Date
Grade 4   Science, Unit VI

MATTER AND ENERGY

B. Energy
   I. Read "Energy to Do Work" pages 147-152; on a separate sheet of paper write your answers to the following in complete sentences.
       1. What is the definition of work?
       2. Why is it *not* work when you push hard against the classroom wall?
       3. In the scientific world, which is more work:

a. To carry a 20-pound load up a flight of stairs, or to

b. Lay a ramp over the stairs and push the 20-pound load up the ramp?

Explain your answer.

II. Read pages 155-159

1. Make a list of 5 examples to show kinetic energy.

2. Make a list of 5 examples to show potential energy.

3. Do the demonstration on page 159 to show the energy of falling water used to do work.

III. Can one form of energy (heat, sound, light, electrical, chemical, atomic, mechanical, potential and kinetic) be changed to another?

Plan a demonstration to prove this.

Name   Date

Grade 4

SIMPLE MACHINES

1. Read booklet: "Machines, Today's Basic Science," pages 233-253.

   List 6 simple machines and give an example of the way in which each one is used.

2. What is friction?

3. Name a useful result of friction.

4. What are harmful effects of friction?

5. How can we reduce friction?

6. Plan a demonstration to show friction occurring. Also demonstrate the reduction of the friction.

7. Plan a demonstration to show how the following simple machine helps to make work easier.

After the child has completed his contract you and he sit down to review it. You are interested in determining primarily whether the child grasped the fundamental concepts, and secondarily, if he has become familiar with relevant data.

Contracts, incidentally should contain experiments or demonstrations for the children to do, as part of their unit of work. In fact, this is a very effective aspect of the entire unit. If the topic does not lend itself to experimentation, models and three-dimensional representations are worth including. For example, atomic structure can best be taught this way.

Find texts which each child can read and understand

So often we doubly penalize the poor reader. He suffers because he has this deficiency, and then he does poorly in other subjects besides reading because he cannot read the necessary textbooks. Science texts are available on many reading levels. If you have children in your class reading below grade level, find texts for them which are on their level, or a bit higher. But it is absurd for us to give a child reading on a third-grade level a sixth-grade text, and expect him to absorb anything from it.

With the advent of Sputnik, our science teaching in many areas of the country advanced—as far as the curriculum is concerned. Whether the children were ready for this advance is a moot question. At any rate, some of the texts which were prepared for them were far above their level of reading comprehension—but were used anyway. By doing this we defeat our own purposes. Worse than that, we turn some of the children off permanently. They become totally disinterested—either in the subject, or in school in general.

If you possibly can, acquire a number of texts for the same grade, covering most of the same work. (It is almost impossible to cover exactly the same curriculum, but you can approximate it.) Assign the text to the individual child, to suit his needs and ability. You can do this for the entire year's work, or you can vary the text with the topic being covered at any particular time.

The poor reader can learn science. We have seen this not once, but many, many times. Not only that, but his confidence is restored, somewhat, by positive experiences. This, in itself, is a goal worth working toward.

A science problem which enables you to work with every child individually

Ideally, every teacher should work with each child on one major science problem he is trying to solve. In some school systems there are Science Fairs, based on this concept. Like learning to drive a car, problem solving is the most important way of studying science.

Even young children can become enthused if you motivate

them—and work with them. These problems may come out of your curriculum, or out of the children's lives. For example, consider topics related to weather (such as keeping a record of how often the Weather Bureau forecasts correctly. To have real fun with this, then compare it with the *Farmers' Almanac.*) Cloud formations, and natural phenomena such as hail, snow, hurricanes or tornadoes make fine projects. The water cycle, too, is of value. Children are curious as to how things work—and projects of this nature can be exciting. Why is an airplane capable of flight? How does an elevator operate? (BEWARE! . . . Observe safety rules and regulations!) Have each child start with a problem, and allow him to solve it himself. Hopefully, he will have to try several hypotheses, but this is not essential. Be sure, though, that the child learns from the work he is doing. Never permit any child to use material or apparatus that is not absolutely safe! Safety first!

Dioramas of prehistoric ages are interesting, but unless the child applies scientific reasoning, they lose some of their value. However, a problem such as trying to determine why dinosaurs disappeared always interests youngsters.

Be sure, too, that the more capable child assumes a more demanding topic.

Some more involved problems might include:

1. How automobile engines work.

2. What is the octane rating in gasoline, and how is it related to performance?

3. How does a telephone work? What is the difference between dialing, and button pushing?

4. Why do moving pictures move? How do they speak? How can we make a "movie" of our own with drawing paper and crayons or pencils and staples?

5. How do tape recorders and cassettes work?

6. Really sophisticated experiments can be done with growing plants.

These are ideas from which your children may choose, although this list should, in no way, limit them.

How should you work with the child?

1. Have him list the problem, and the method he proposes using on an index card. Go over this with him, question him to be sure

he knows what he is doing, and offer suggestions if you feel they are necessary. (But only if you feel the necessity.)

2. Give a certain length of time, in which he is to do the work. Discuss it again to be sure the child is on the right track.

3. Then have the problem completed, and have a final conference to check the results. Be sure the child draws his own conclusions. Do not tell him the answers. Have him tell them to you.

Children may work with each other

You may feel your children are able to work on more complex problems if they work in groups. This is good, for it establishes a situation more like the ones they will encounter when they have completed their schooling, and are earning a living.

Be sure that any child in the group carries his or her weight. Often children will relax and "let George do it." For this particular work, that idea is completely unsuitable. Question each child independently, to be sure he or she is doing his or her bit. In this type of situation, pairing a bright child with a slower one can benefit both children, providing each contributes.

When children are choosing their topics, first have them select the topic, and consider whether it needs two or more people to solve it successfully. We saw one group do a sensational project on getting energy from the sun. They constructed many devices which did just this. Four youngsters worked on it, and it was obvious that all four knew exactly what was going on. The apparatus they made indicated a high level of sophistication.

Building an interest in ecology

Not too long ago, there was a show called "Stop the World, I Want to Get Off." It's a cute idea, but there's little chance of our having any choice—in this generation, at any rate. But our earth is rapidly becoming a place from which people will want to escape. We have to do something about it. As teachers, the first thing we have to do is teach our children to be aware of the environment, what is happening to it, and what we can do to prevent it from being destroyed.

We are faced with a formidable number of problems. We are polluting the air we breathe, the waters which surround us, and the land on which we live. We are killing off animals such as the blue whale, and diminishing our supplies of wood, coal and oil at rates that stagger the imagination. But probably the most severe problem is that of population increase. If we continue at the rate at which we are going, there will be 8 billion people living on this planet by the year 2020. How will they be fed or housed adequately? Why are we concerned? Because our children, those we are teaching now, will still be alive and hopefully well by 2020. Our children and their children must be made aware of the powder keg on which we are all sitting.

There are various ways to teach ecology. But even the first grade is not too soon to begin. The little ones can collect newspapers and aluminum cans for recycling. The older ones can study what litter and nonusable trash is doing to our landscapes. The "car graveyards" are a particular affront. While we plunder the earth for more ores, metals from these rusting cars sink back into the soil, slowly and valuelessly.

Children should be taught the value of animals and the tasks they do in the ecological scheme. They should realize the need for trees and plants to return oxygen to the environment. All of these ideas are important, if our children are to grow up with an understanding of the value of the earth, the only home we have.

Have each child do an ecological project of his own. It need not be a complicated one, but it should show an understanding and a feeling for the environment. This will have more of an effect on him than talking about the situation, but not doing anything.

Make each child responsible for a living thing in the classroom

Tying in with the work in ecology, we should teach a respect for, and a reverence of, living things. When you make a child feel a responsibility for a plant or an animal, you develop these emotions in him. Have the child select whatever thing he wishes—be it plant or animal. In the plant kingdom, bulbs are very rewarding, and can be observed from the earliest growth. Planting seeds is very worthwhile, and gives the child the chance to learn how to handle them. Have the youngster vary the conditions under which his plant lives, to find those which are most advantageous for it. But be sure the child understands it is his, and his responsibility to care for it.

Animals may range from fish (goldfish or guppies are fine), to turtles. Again, be sure the conditions are suited to the animals' well-being.

Another project to consider is planting trees. Since trees such as the mimosa or weeping willow grow remarkably quickly, the children are able to see results of their labors within several years after planting. Honey locust trees, too, are fast growing. Have the children select the type of trees they want to plant. Place a marker near them to commemorate the date of planting, and as a reminder of the class which planted them. This leads into a fine lesson on the importance of trees in the environment, and how each person can make a contribution, if he so desires. If your school has no area in which to plant trees, perhaps one can be created. Before mentioning this to the children, speak to the custodian about it.

What are you going to be when you grow up?

Choosing a career is one of the most important decisions anyone must make in his entire lifetime, and yet we do painfully little career education in the years we have the children with us. There are so many possible careers in science and related areas that some time and attention given to it may be of tremendous benefit to your children.

If you find a child is interested in this area, or gifted, do not miss the opportunity to call this to his attention, and in some way, to point him in the right direction. You may wish to have the class make a list of all of the careers they can think of which are related to science or health. Then have them choose one, and do research in it—to find out what the career actually consists of—what the person does on a day-to-day basis. In addition, introduce the children to occupations they do not list. Technical careers are excellent for many of them—because there is a great need for technically-trained people—and this training can be gotten in two-year college courses. When we say science, we do not necessarily mean Ph.D.s, or M.D.s. The variety of other vocations is very large, offering a great deal of choice to the young person.

Survival lessons

There are certain lessons which should be taught to every child—since they determine whether or not he will survive, and live to become a healthy adult.

1. Tell the children, "Never, but never, put a plastic material over your head, your nose or your mouth. The plastic, even if it is very lightweight, may get stuck to the mucous membranes of your nose and mouth, preventing you from breathing. You would suffocate."

2. Discuss behavior during an electrical storm. If you are out of doors during a storm, when there is lightning, never go under a tree. A car is a safe place, because it is grounded, but since a tree is tall, lightning often strikes it. Furthermore, don't touch anyone under a tree, since the lightning can travel along your arms.

3. Discuss electrical currents, and the need to avoid touching any switch at all while standing in water. People have been known to be electrocuted while in the bathtub, because they turned the light on or off. The same is true of pumping water out of a flooded basement. If you are standing in water, avoid touching the switch. If you must turn it on, get out of the water.

4. Instruct them "Never take any pills of any kind, unless you are told to do so by your physician, or your parents. You have no idea what chemicals a pill may contain, and how you will react to them."

5. "Never take any injection, no matter what it is, unless it is given to you by your doctor or nurse. The injection may easily kill you—if it is something to which you are allergic, and you may not know whether you are allergic to it or not."

If you have a child in your class who is a slow learner, make sure he, too, learns these rules. Review them with him again and again. They may easily save his life.

Narcotics, alcohol and cigarette smoking

Certainly we cannot omit mention of the topics of narcotics, alcohol and cigarette smoking in the section on survival.

Each of these areas claims many lives. Yet a child never realizes he may become one of the victims.

Read with the class the surgeon general's warning on every pack of cigarettes. Have them tell you exactly what it means. Then divide your class into two groups—and work with those who already smoke, and those who do not. You may want to concentrate with children who want to quit, but can't. (We have found 12-year-olds in this category.)

Discuss the difference between social drinking, *for adults* and the drinking which leads to alcoholism. You may wish to call attention to current research—articles and television programs—which bring this problem into focus.

In regard to narcotics, even young children must be taught to avoid trying anything. They should be made to understand that they put nothing in their mouths except what their parents give them. As they get older, you will want to discuss with the children the danger of experimenting. This desire to be one of the peer group is very important. *If you find you have a child who is already involved in the use of any drug, make sure you take action on it. Either notify your supervisor, the guidance counselor, or the parents—depending on whatever your school policy is. NEVER, NEVER IGNORE IT.*

Summary

In teaching science, try to develop, rather than stifle, the child's curiosity. One of the best ways to do this is by questioning the class, rather than by giving them information. Have the children figure things out—for themselves—whenever possible.

Each child should do experiments frequently. These need not be complex, but they should enable the child to solve a problem, or to answer a question, as a result of the work he does. Try to help the child to develop the method of thinking called "scientific reasoning," or the "scientific method," and show him how he may apply it to situations in his everyday life.

You can individualize the curriculum by the use of contracts, as well as by experimentation. It is also advisable to obtain textbooks on many reading levels, so that the child who is reading below grade level can achieve in science, even if he is handicapped in reading.

Establish, once a year, a major science problem on which each child works individually or with a group. Be sure this is a true problem-solving activity, fully motivated, then researched, hypothesized and followed through. This will require much individualization of instruction, but may be one of the most significant activities you can initiate.

Building an interest in ecology and in saving our planet from destruction may be one of the most important topics you cover—in the long run. It may be personalized by giving every child in the class a responsibility for the care of one living thing.

Discussing a child's future occupation with him can possibly affect his entire life, and should certainly be introduced—no matter what the age or grade of the child.

We conclude with a series of lessons which should be taught to every child, on his level, of course, by every teacher. We have named them Survival Lessons—and they can play a part in saving his life. Be sure to teach them, regardless of the child's age, for he may never learn them otherwise; and these lessons are indeed necessary for his very survival.

11

Individualizing instruction to foster creativity in art, music, home economics, industrial arts and health education

Why are all of these areas—so unlike in content and activity—linked together in one chapter? Actually, it is because one fundamental principle governs instruction in all of them. It is this: motivate the child, give him basic instructions, be sure he understands them, point him in the right direction, and let him go off on his own. Allow him to discover for himself that he enjoys basketball, but hates football, or that she loves to paint, but can't stand working with clay. These classes are the opportunities children get to really express themselves in non-verbal fashion. They should be able to go from one area to another, from one medium to a second or even a third, without being told, "You must do this, today, right now—or you will fail." The name of the game should be self-expression. Can you think of a greater service we can do for children than to help them to find their talents? Can you see how bringing music into a child's life may enrich him forever? Can you, if you are really interested in a child's development, ignore these activities which will bring him pleasure, and possibly much more—throughout his entire life?

Credit Official Photograph, Bd. of Ed., N.Y.C.

Figure 11-1

Encouraging each child to explore his talents

Not everyone of us is talented, and fewer of us recognize our own talents or gifts. That is where you, the teacher, are so important. Starting when the children are very young, you can actually make them feel gifted, by simple means. For example, give them drawing paper, one color paint (a bright, attractive shade), or crayons, and ask them to illustrate "happiness" for you. Discuss the topic, and the use of color and line to bring the idea across. Even point out the use of upward lines, such as the simple diagram of a smile. After the discussion, give the children free rein. Some of the results will be very fine, others not so good. But comment favorably on some aspect of each paper, and hang it up, unless a child asks you not to. The second time, use "sadness," and follow the same procedure. You will discover the children will become accustomed to working in this way. As they work, walk around the room, offering suggestions and assistance. "This is excellent," you say, "would you like to make this line a little longer?" When you ask, really mean it as a question. Some children do not like to have their work changed at all. Those who are talented will show up as cream in a bottle of non-homogenized milk. The child talented in art will usually enjoy this assignment. Others can get something out of it, too. But for the youngsters whose area of creativity this is, this type of open assignment gives them the "carte blanche" to go ahead, yet directs their thoughts and energies.

Credit Official Photograph, Bd. of Ed., N.Y.C.

Figure 11-2

In all of the subject areas—music, home economics, industrial arts, health education—follow the same basic pattern. If a child is playing volleyball, and you can see a way of assisting him, call him over and give him some instruction. But play it cool; very, very cool. Not a long lecture, but short, to-the-point directions. Instead of teaching the same details to every child, give each youngster, individually, what he, personally, needs.

Credit Official Photograph, Bd. of Ed., N.Y.C.

Figure 11-3

Giving each child a jumping-off place

Very often an adult will say, "I wish I could have played the drums when I was a kid." If you can, try to give every youngster a "tasting sample," of an instrument he'd like to try. Not everyone wants to play the drums—although many do. But it's cute to see a little bit of a girl bowing a huge cello. Perhaps its appeal is because it's so big, and she's so small.

Media are important, and a chance to try everything is almost a child's dream. Perhaps that is too ambitious, but even if you come close, it's worthwhile. This includes charcoal, pencil, pastels, crayons, oils, water colors—and everything else you can think of. It means working with clay or papier mâché, or even homemade mixtures of salt, flour and water which can be used to make a relatively inexpensive "dough." (If you wish to experiment with this, food coloring makes it far more attractive than if left in its natural state.)

In the area of industrial arts, the list is huge, too. Metals, wood, cardboard, wire, glass—and how about aluminum cans or even foil? (The cans are far less expensive.) Of course, this introduction to the child must include teaching him some basic techniques, so that he knows what he is doing.

In home economics, some of our young adults have returned to baking their own bread, and even growing their own vegetables. Others never left. But for those who are uninitiated, all of the skills—cooking, sewing, knitting, embroidering, crocheting—can be sources of creativity and satisfaction. We have seen little ones get great pleasure from making horse reins and creating huge chains of chewing gum wrappers. The joy of cooking may be combined with the desire to show affection, for some people. But they must know how to cook to do so. "Mrs. Karlin, I made these cookies just for you. I spent all day on them. I hope you like them. They're Toll House cookies. You know how much work they are." The speaker, incidentally, was not a child, but a seventy-year-young lady, whose gifts of love are always things she bakes.

We have already mentioned exposing children to various musical instruments. How can we neglect to mention the guitar, which has captured the imagination of so many of the young people? But don't ignore the recorder, and even the harmonica, as well as the instruments found in orchestras and bands.

Singing, too, offers children an opportunity to use their talents, and to enjoy doing so.

The same policy should apply to sports. Why do children learn so many team sports, and so few which can be played independently? In Australia, for example, youngsters learn to play tennis from the time they are very young. (The number of champions they produce reflects this.) If you can introduce your children to skating, to golf, or to bowling, as well as to basketball and baseball, you can enrich their lives greatly.)

Even young children can become enthused about a sport. Many famous athletes report starting in their sports before they were in their teens. Most of them began in the streets. A number can thank their parents. However, if you are involved in a particular sport, and you can bring it to your children, give them a chance to partake. Wealthy children get this type of exposure in private camps. Why shouldn't you give your pupils the opportunity?

Don't be discouraged if some of your youngsters appear to be relatively poorly coordinated. Even if they are, the introduction is just what the word implies, and the next time they meet the sport, they will have some familiarity with it.

Other children have parents who play golf or tennis, or who bowl or ride horseback. When you have discussed the sport, and given the child a bit of instruction, perhaps the parents will take over, and involve the child in their plans.

Sampling new ideas

We recently saw an industrial arts display, in which the featured attractions were the many lovely items made from used, empty aluminum cans. These ranged from ashtrays to clever ornaments.

One creative art teacher showed a design made by pasting tubes made of white paper on a dark background. The tubes varied in size—but were about the length of a cigarette—regular, kingsized, etc. They were used to form a picture of a Greek temple.

Some of the home economics teachers have worked with the prepared foods and done variations on them. Using a cake mix, for example, they have created really superb cakes.

As you initiate projects, work with each child on those he enjoys. If he is all thumbs, perhaps you can find something he can do without becoming frustrated. Papier mâché, inexpensive to make, may be sculpted into abstract shapes, and then painted. It's fun to do, and the results can be amazing. Collages are another excellent device for children who do not like drawing or painting. Select a topic and have the children find pictures from magazines related to it. They then cut out the pictures and arrange them to form an attractive composite. Next, they paste them on a base, shellac or varnish it, and it is ready for display. The base may be a sheet of cardboard, a wastebasket, a tray or anything else they wish to decorate.

In all areas, keep your eyes open for ideas you can use with your children. You will see them everywhere—in advertisements, in variety stores, in commercial products, in store windows, in magazines or books. A recipe for the best candy we ever ate was on a package of cereal—but it took a highly creative teacher to bring it into school to have the youngsters prepare it.

What to do to start off the child who feels he has no talent

No matter which activity you initiate, there will be some child who feels he has no talent, and will be reluctant to try it—if you permit him to withdraw from the situation and watch. Don't! After you have motivated an activity, and of course every activity needs motivation, then go around and help every child to get started. This may mean giving the child more ideas, or teaching him skills, but whatever he needs, it is usually possible to get him to begin. If this seems impossible, find another activity for him. If he sits and watches the others, he develops poor attitudes, "Why should I bother?" Or he may think, "I can't do this, so it's stupid to try."

You may find that other children can work with him, and that a pair, or even a larger group, will benefit all of the children.

In some areas, children lack manual dexterity, or a physical lack of coordination may be at the root of the problem. Some little ones have difficulty controlling their drawing, for example, or cannot handle even simple tools. Then you have to develop projects which they can do, and which, incidentally, may help them to improve physically. Children who are overweight will often do anything to avoid physical training. They play sick, they hide, they stay out of school, they bring in medical notes asking for them to be excused. In the latter case, incidentally, there is nothing you can do. You cannot have a child do exercises if he has medical permission to be excluded.

Talent is almost a state of mind. If a child has had a number of successful experiences, he will not be afraid to take on new challenges. If, on the other hand, everything he has ever done is down-graded, he looks at life from that viewpoint.

James B. was such a child. In the seventh grade he had a reading score of 3.4. He was rarely able to express himself adequately. But he could draw. Yet even in his art class, he was doing nothing. The district supervisor, on a class visit one day, saw James sitting, talking with some of his friends. The supervisor knew James, and said, "But James, you draw so well! How come you aren't creating something beautiful?" James shrugged.

"I don't understand," the supervisor continued. "You did that magnificent poster for me." It had been one to rival Peter Max in color and imagination.

No answer.

The gentleman pressed. "James, what's the matter?"

Finally came the answer. "That teacher doesn't like my stuff. It wasn't 'right.' "

Here was a boy who did have talent, but it was being wasted because the teacher's approach was a negative one. In art, we can let them do it "their way." In fact, that is what we should be striving for, isn't it?

Avoiding negative criticism

In all of the fields we are discussing in this chapter, negative criticism is deadly. It's deadly most of the time, but in the creative areas it can kill any talent a child might have. One little girl was told she was a "listener." When asked to define it, she said, "The teacher said that when everyone sang, I should listen." Perhaps this teacher felt she was being kind. Or amusing. Actually, the child loved to sing, but never did because of the fear of being embarrassed again.

In your lifetime, haven't you, at one time or another, been discouraged by a chance remark? Haven't you had someone hurt you, really hurt you, deep down inside, because of some tidbit of this nature? It might have been criticism of a piece of your work, or of you as a person, but whatever, doesn't it rankle?

Realize though, that you can do the same thing, inadvertently.

If you ask a little one, "What are you drawing?" and he says "A horse," and you answer "It's very nice, but it doesn't look like a horse," what effect do you have on the child? For purposes of the creative areas, wouldn't you agree that a noncommittal reply to any statement is far better? Besides that, if you visit museums of art, you will find that, so often, artists, whose work is on exhibit, have drawn horses that you wouldn't take for horses, anyway. So if the child answers, "A horse," your best bet is to reply, "Very interesting," or "A horse, ah!" (said without any incredulity) or something which, if it were said to you, would not upset you.

Sometimes, drawing, music, or sports can supply an emotional catharsis which the child may need. (They can, and do, the same thing for adults.) We know of one very frustrated woman who, as she ran out of her office in a very upset condition, announced, "I'm going to play tennis. I really need to hit a few." What did she mean—people or tennis balls?

The child who can use these outlets is indeed fortunate, for he has found a socially-acceptable way of getting out some of his anger. If he paints a horrible, ugly scene, perhaps he feels some relief. But then, what happens if his teacher says to him, "That's a poor choice of color. Why did you use all those blacks and purples?"

Whenever you want to give helpful criticism or instruction, ask a child if he wants help. Our friend, James, interpreted the teacher's desire to help him with hostility. If a youngster is asked, his attitude in answering will reveal to you whether or not he really wants your assistance.

For talent to flourish, sincere encouragement is the keynote

How do you sincerely encourage children? That will depend on your personality. If you can be enthusiastic without being gushy, fine. If a child is a superlative ball player, he will be aware of it, but words, spoken quietly and privately, may convince him that he has a future playing baseball in high school, and later in college, or possibly professionally.

If you feel something is worthy of note, make mention of it, but never at the expense of the others.

Giving individualized instruction helps, too. "The most significant thing I learned in cooking class," one adult recently told us, "was said by the teacher in an aside. 'Don't be afraid to experiment,' she said, 'What you are cooking can always be remade if necessary, but most of the time the experiments are big improvements over the originals.' " This is not true of everyone's cooking, but the speaker is renowned for her culinary talents.

When you find children who show they have talent, it is possible to have them help you a great deal in your classroom. For instance, you may wish to have several class artists, who will do many of the posters and charts which you require. In the lower grades, the class artists, or the entire class, may illustrate new words or new ideas from any subject area. When one of the authors taught general science, a young man in her class made a series of charts illustrating the various branches of science—from anthropology to zoology. The young man returned to visit the school years later—a still young, but successful, artist. He was very

Credit Official Photograph, Bd. of Ed., N.Y.C.

Figure 11-4

excited to see his work still on display. "I've had other charts drawn, many times, but none could compare with these," she told him.

Another sincere means of encouragement is to display the children's work. Your room can be a constantly changing art gallery. If you assign two children to act as bulletin board monitors, they will do the actual physical work of putting up and taking down the work on display. (If you assign this task to children who are not particularly talented, they may get satisfaction from this activity.) Everything you have put up need not be perfect, but it should have some merit. Don't have junk hung around the room. It lowers everyone's standards. If you have a great deal of good work, you can offer to decorate the hallways. This will endear you to the administration.

To encourage creativity in home economics or industrial arts, the same policy of exhibiting good work is most worthwhile. It is possible to hold any number of shows, exhibits, fairs or the like to display the students' products. We have seen luncheons, and teas, and "Fathers' Nights," (at which the boys showed their fathers how they used the industrial arts equipment in the school).

In music and sports, excellence is encouraged, and talent nurtured by programs which give the children the opportunity to show what they can do. Gymkanas (exhibits of various physical activities), team games, even field days, are ways of doing this. Concerts, of course, do the same thing. In every area, when work is put on display, children are encouraged to try harder.

When a child does any piece of work at home, and wishes to show it to the class, he should certainly be encouraged to do so. One little one brought in a magnificent scene. She had created it by forming a picture using peas, beans, (both dried), weeds and various forms of macaroni. She'd worked under the direction of her mother. The youngsters were so enthralled they asked that the mother be invited to teach the class. She did, and the results were lovely. Everyone involved was enriched.

Introducing the world of art and music to your children

It has been our observation that most children have not been given enough exposure in the areas of art and music appreciation. While we are not advocating the memorization of the names and masterpieces of famous artists, we do believe each child should be introduced to some of the world-famous paintings, sculpture, and pieces of music. You will find that some youngsters will be drawn to this more than others, but we have seen very surprising results when we showed reproductions of Picasso's works to a group of fourth graders. They loved many of them, and after we discussed what the artist was trying to do, some of them were for trying to draw their own abstractions immediately.

One really has to discover these worlds for himself, and often this is at a later age than elementary school. However, when the person meets the works of an artist or composer later, it is like meeting an old friend. Your personal enthusiasm will make the difference. If you are obviously enthralled, some of the children will be, too. If you are phlegmatic about it, they will be, too. Expect this, and watch what happens. You'll find it fascinating.

Do not start with very deep material, in either case. Find, even among the masterworks, paintings or musical selections the children will enjoy. If your taste is very sophisticated, choose for them carefully, because you can turn them off, too. Colorful music or art is most appropriate for beginning these areas of appreciation. We think of such selections as the William Tell Overture, Schubert's Serenade, the operettas of Gilbert and Sullivan for starters. Or Mona Lisa (because they probably have heard of it), the works of Vincent van Gogh, El Greco or Picasso in the field of art. In sculpture, Rodin, or Michelangelo, the ancient Greeks or the mobiles of Calder would stimulate the children's interest.

Your children will react differently. For those who manifest an interest in the subject, give them material to read or to listen to. Arrange, if you can, for museum visits. Public libraries often have excellent collections of records or tapes which the youngsters may borrow. If at all possible, try to arrange for trips to concerts. If you cannot find the time for this, perhaps there are parents who would be willing to contribute their time to such projects.

You may wish to have the children bring records from home. Also, have them sing songs in foreign languages.

You can find time to play records for them, as background music, while they are hanging up their clothing and attendance is being taken. You may find this will have a beneficial effect if the selections you choose are melodious, but serene.

Opening the youngsters' eyes to the wonders of the world around them

The advent of television has made the world into one big village, with happenings on the other side of the globe as easily seen as if they were next door. Unless we point out the wonders of these everyday occurences, our children may grow up without feeling any of them. They may just be taken for granted. The question is "Can we allow the children to do so?" Even in terms of our daily life, there are wonders—if one is aware of them. For example, no one need iron today. If a housewife chooses permanent press items when she purchases clothing and household linens, she need never have the ironing chore again. But it wasn't always this way. In the same regard, there have been changes in art, music, in all areas. If these are not considered, then the flavor of the times in which we live, of constantly new developments, is lost.

Why are these wonders important? For one thing, they may lead to the careers these children will enter. It has been said, many times, that numerous jobs of the 1980's are still to be created—that they are unknown today. By watching new developments, children become aware of the new fields, and possibly they themselves lean in those directions. There are careers in sports, today, which are brand new. Recreation directors, for example, help people to find "their thing" in the area of sports.

How to teach, even if you are not particularly talented in any of these areas

Teaching, in and of itself, is an art. If you are a talented teacher, you need not have other gifts. In other words, you can teach art, yet not be an artist yourself. You can teach music, yet not be of concert caliber. The same holds true in home economics, industrial arts or health education. How then, you are asking, do you go about this?

First, motivation. You have to take the time and make the effort to really motivate the children. Motivation is more than showing them a sample, and saying, "This is what we are going to do today." It is relating the project to their lives, and making them see a particular use for it. It is giving the youngster a chance to create or make something he wants, but cannot buy. It is showing him that he can get satisfaction from making and then using an item, or seeing it used. Little ones enjoy making gifts for their parents. We have seen first-graders bursting with pride at the first card they write, and also first-year high school students reacting almost the same way—for the same reason.

Second, give good instructions. In this, you may need help from another source. Perhaps there is another teacher. In some cases it may be a pupil, and in others a parent. But make sure that the children understand just how to proceed.

1. Take nothing for granted. If a teaspoon of sugar is to be added, and you haven't reviewed it lately, make sure the child knows what a teaspoon is. If you tell a child to use a plane, check to make sure he is able to use it. If a ball is to be thrown underhand, ask someone to demonstrate just how this is done.

2. Your instructions should be step by step. This, too, appears to be very fundamental, but we know of one case where a recipe called for two preparations, but at no point directed the baker to put the two together. As a result a cake was baked, which contained no flour. It was a delicious shell.

3. The instructions should be in writing—so that the child may refer to them when necessary. When we are doing something, we often need to check. Sometimes, this is again and again. There is security in having the steps listed for quick referral.

4. Word them as simply as you know how. This is worthwhile, even in physical education. If you wish to develop an exercise program, it is easier to remember it, for some youngsters, if they see each exercise given a name, and then written down—in the order in which they are to be done.

5. If practice is necessary, leave time for it. In some instances, this can make all the difference in the world. In others, it is not needed.

Third, have on hand all of the materials they will be using. It is a nuisance to be doing something, and have it interrupted for lack of materials.

Fourth, do not allow too much time for any one activity. Children get bored easily. Give them as much time as seems necessary. When you see that they are getting tired, instruct them to finish up, or put their work away, to be returned to at another time.

Fifth, leave room for individual interpretation. Even in cases where choice may be annoying, give the child the chance to make his own variations. Rigidity of thinking has limited many, many adults. If we can draw our youngsters away from it, we do them a service.

Sixth, if a child wishes them, and you can, give him at least some helpful hints; or full instruction if he needs and wants it. If you aren't capable of helping him, try to find someone who can. Tell him you are trying, so that he doesn't think you are ignoring his needs.

Seventh, if you find you are not getting good results, check into the reasons why. You may have overlooked something, when writing up the instructions. Or you may have made an out-and-out error. For whatever reason, check into the cause.

Eighth, if you find some of the children enjoy the activity, there is no reason why they cannot repeat it if they wish to. So often, a practice session is well worthwhile. If, on the other hand, they have "had it," allow them to proceed to something else.

With these ideas in mind, we believe your teaching of an activity may be made easier. Where can you find different projects? In a variety of places:

1. In courses you have taken in college in methods of teaching this particular area. Check your notes. You may find much you have forgotten, which can prove to be very useful.

2. By observing, talking with and about other teachers. Your supervisors, for instance, often may offer ideas because they have seen the teaching of many teachers, both in your school and in others. Over the lunch table, many ideas are exchanged, some of which are very, very worthwhile, because one tends to discuss the things with which he has been successful.

3. In workshops given by your Board of Education, or by colleges or universities. One art teacher got the idea for doing orange-crate stage settings at just such a workshop. He came back skeptical, but tried it. Some of the children took to it well, but one child made it his own. It was practically his salvation, for this child was handicapped, and desperately needed something he could do well. He became famous throughout the school and then in the community as a result of his work on one particular set.

Summary

Creativity in art, music, home economics, industrial arts and health education depends on many factors. Children must be motivated, given the basic instructions, and then handed materials and time to experiment and to grow and develop. Almost every youngster, if sufficiently encouraged, will pursue one particular area, and become comfortable with it. However, he needs a place from which to start. A brilliant sculptor may miss his calling completely if he never has the opportunity to try. We can and should supply many such opportunities in our classes.

By discovering and introducing new ideas, we make learning exciting—for both the children and ourselves. In dealing with youngsters who feel they have no talent, our encouragement and individual instruction can play a very large role. Negative criticism should and must be avoided. The teacher cannot afford the luxury of a sharp tongue. Negative remarks can devastate a child—without even being intended to do so.

The subjects of art and music appreciation sometimes have been ignored, yet represent areas which can benefit your children tremendously. Even if you feel you are not a particularly talented person yourself, you can bring out the best in your children—which is, in and of itself, a very great art.

12

Individualization of instruction in teaching children work and behavior skills

We have discussed individualized instruction in the various subject areas. However, we have not discussed in specific detail skills which will enable the children to succeed in the academic environment, where most of our youngsters will find themselves, in one school or another, for many years to come. These skills include how to study in general, and how to prepare for tests in particular. These topics will be covered in this chapter. We then move on to working with the child who has not been able to get the maximum or even minimum benefits from the school situation. He is the youngster who requires the additional attention and instruction you can give him—far more than his more capable, or more accomplishing, classmate. He may have problems adjusting to the class because he has not learned to make friends, or he may be disruptive, but, whatever the reason, he is in need of your TLC (Tender Loving Care).

This type of individualization requires an emotional input on your part. It involves your being involved. It asks that you see the youngsters not as problems, but as having problems. And that you want to help them to solve these problems. Most teachers do want to help, but really don't know how. It is with them in mind that we write these pages. How many times we have heard the words,

"I wish I could do something with Milly. I just don't know, though, what I can do." Perhaps these pages will be of assistance.

Teaching a child how to study

The greatest thing you can do for a child is to teach him how to read. Coming in a very close second is teaching him how to study. It is our estimate that 90 percent of the children in our schools have never been taught the techniques involved in learning material which a teacher has presented to them. We send them home with assignments such as "Study pages 10 to 20. You're having a test on this tomorrow." But nary a word about how to study those pages. Or we say, "Read Chapter IV and answer the questions for homework. You'll be getting a test on this material." Here we're coming closer—but still not there.

It is common knowledge that each child is different from the rest of his classmates and learns at a different rate of speed. We gear our teaching to these varying rates. But when it comes to a realization of how to study, those differences are ignored! This is where individualized instruction comes in. We have to help each youngster find his way! Without it, he is really lost. Many do learn how to study without formal instruction, but those who do not are doomed to academic oblivion.

How do you study? How did those who were close to you? Each person has to find the right method for him. We are offering a series of techniques. Perhaps with your individualized instruction, you can reach every child with one of these:

1. When you teach a topic, be sure each child has a written record of every important point in the lesson.

    a. You can write them on the board and have him copy them.

    b. A class secretary can write them as you dictate.

    c. You can give out rexographed material.

If you write the notes on the board, be sure every child copies them. If you use a secretary, you can easily walk around, checking to be sure each child is writing them. However, the secretary must write legibly.

2. Tell the children, "If you learn every item on this list, you will do very well on your tests. You have nothing to worry about,

if you can learn this material." Motivate them—and keep your word. Why not? If everyone gets 100 percent, that's perfect teaching. It won't happen often, but if it does, it's gratifying.

3. Now—the big question: How do they go home and learn the material? Tell them there are many ways to do this, and that they have to find the way which is best for them. You are going to present them with some techniques with which they should experiment. Introduce the material which follows by discussing the need to develop the ability to study. Tell them if they can master this, it will help them for many years to come. Stress the fact that different people learn differently. In the techniques which follow, we are using three different sensory approaches. The first is silent reading—which uses the sense of sight. The second is writing, which uses both the senses of sight and touch. The third is a combination, too, using both the senses of sight and hearing. It has been found that there are certain people who must hear words in order to remember them. Others can do so by reading. One of the authors discovered, while in college, that in order to remember, writing helped her greatly.

Be positive in your approach. Convince the children they can learn to study, and they will benefit from this all of their lives. You may duplicate this material, and distribute it to the children.

How-to-study guide

For each method the same beginning steps are used:

1. Read everything you must learn very carefully.

2. Think about it.

3. Be sure you understand it—before trying to really learn it.

4. If you don't understand it, ask your teacher or another person to explain it to you. As you grow older, you may have to find the explanation in books.

5. Take the material you have to learn and divide it into small segments of from four to six items. We call these "groups."

6. Give each group a title. What is the main thought? What links the group together? In what ways are the items related? (As you progress in school, your groups may contain more items, but otherwise the technique is the same.)

Now, how do you make these groups part of your personal knowledge? How do you learn them?

A. By reading:

Read one group at a time. Think about it. Read every item over, again and again, until you feel you know it.

Then go on to the next group. Do the same thing.

When you have learned every group, put your papers away and see if you can go through the entire list—group by group, then item by item. Test yourself by doing it in writing.

B. By writing:

Instead of reading one group at a time, make a list of the groups. Then read the entire batch of material and put the paper away. See how many items you can place under each group. Write in as many as you can. When you have written in as many as possible, check your work against the original listing. Fill in each group.

Then write the list of groups, and write each item in the first group. Write it again, completely, from the original. Write it a third time. Then test yourself, by trying to write it completely, without looking at the previous list. Keep writing until you are able to write each item in a group. Then go on to the next group.

This method takes lots of scrap paper, and patience. But it is better because you cannot fool yourself into thinking you have learned something—until you can write it, fully.

C. By reading aloud:

This method consists of reading each group aloud, item by item, again and again. Then test yourself, by writing the groups and each item, to see whether you have learned what you are studying. Relearn any group which gives you trouble.

D. Another technique for learning a topic is to teach it to another person. Have you not found that if you teach you learn at the same time? You cannot slur over anything, and you must understand it—before you can teach it.

To teach, you have to take a topic apart, divide it into smaller segments, teach it, and put it together again. This almost always assures you of understanding the subject. It points out any areas which are missing.

E. Still another technique for studying is to work with another person, and to question each other. This, too, is excellent, because it involves questioning, and therefore, thinking of responses.

How to learn from a text

1. If you have a chapter to study, outline it.

2. Each section usually has one main idea, with a number of items to make it clear, or to explain it. Find this central idea and then list underneath it the points relating to it. Then go on to the next main idea, and its point. Do this for the entire chapter.

3. When you have outlined the chapter, study it by one of the methods listed above.

4. You may wish to change each section idea to a question. Then, when you study, you answer the series of questions you have developed.

5. Of course, this means there will be many questions to each chapter. Do not let this frighten you. In this way, you will really cover all of the required material.

Using the study methods

After you have taught the children these techniques, encourage them to use them. Give them some material to learn, and tell them they will be tested on it. Do this several times. Some children will still not be able to do well, and it is these, of course, who need your individualized instruction. Go over the techniques, step-by-step; try to determine where the child is not following the instructions.

Reviewing in class

In order to have review lessons which give the maximum benefits to your students, have them write the answers to questions you ask them. When you review orally (and most of us did, and do), some of the children participate, but not all of them. If they write, perhaps every child won't answer all of the questions, but you can easily check this by walking around the room.

The review may serve as an indicator to you that individualized instruction is needed on a particular point by a certain child, or certain children. You can cover the material again, with them, or you can have another student do so if you have one who is capable. If you try this system, please be careful not to embarrass any child with a learning deficiency. Children may be rather harsh, in such a situation. Be sure you choose youngsters who will be pleased to assist, and who have positive feelings for others.

Specific teaching for testing

Would you like to have your children study and do well on your tests? You can, if you follow this relatively simple procedure: Tell them they will be tested and what work will be covered. Give the material to them in the form of review notes. Assure them they will pass with flying colors if they learn everything you give them. Point out to them that you are simplifying their studying, and that, in the future, they may have to do the outlining for themselves.

Let us say that you give notes with 50 different items in ten groups. (This is a challenge to most children.) Select from those 50 items about 4/5 of the test. For the other 1/5, put in questions which require interpretation. Using this method helps those youngsters who have problems with reading. They can become familiar with the vocabulary, and learn to read the material before they are faced with it on a test.

We wish to point out that we believe children are in school to learn. They should have every chance to be creative, and need opportunities to express themselves. They deserve to be able to ventilate some of their feelings and emotions. But, first and foremost, they are in school to learn. The methods we have outlined will help them to retain material. Your questioning will help them to use it. Class discussions will help them to apply it. We bring this point out because we have met teachers who believe all children need in school is a place for self-expression. While this is one of their needs, and should be one of our aims, it cannot be our major one. Our major aim must be to teach them.

Have you ever taken a college course, and studied for hours—only to find that the instructor pulled questions out of a hat, asking about topics which he never covered? How did you feel? It is to avoid such a situation that we suggest the method above. Give the children the material you want them to learn. Help them to learn it. Test them, and then reward them for what they have learned. We ask you to try this technique, and to experiment with it. It will bring both you and the children satisfaction.

We learned about this method from Christopher, a high school senior. "When I was a freshman I had a social studies teacher who did lots of exciting things. We had debates, and I remember we went on trips. But we didn't know what we were supposed to learn, so we asked him to make a list of all of the things he felt we had to know. We were friends, and we thought we could ask him for this. He went for the idea, and gave us one long list of questions. Then he told us that since these were the main concepts and facts he hoped we would learn, he would take most of the test from the list. We went home and worked like dogs. But almost all of us got in the 90's. We thought he was a really nice guy, and that he was too easy—but as I look at it now, I still remember most of the stuff that was on that list."

How to study for any test

Teach the children to study for tests (if they were not given review sheets) in the following manner: Tell them:

1. Be sure you know exactly what material you will be held accountable for. If you have any questions, ask your teacher. The more specific this information is, the easier it is for you to study.

2. Be sure you read every question carefully. Sometimes, if you read very quickly, you miss the point of the question. It is very important that you pay attention to what you are reading.

3. Be sure you do not miss any question. If there is more than one page, find out how many pages there are, and make certain you have all of them. Pages may sometimes stick together. It would be a shame to do poorly in a test because you overlooked some of the questions.

4. Keep note of the time. Don't allow so much time for the first questions that you never get to those at the end. Sometimes it is better to go through a test, and answer those questions you know than to chance missing some of them.

5. Unless you are told that you will be penalized (and be sure the definition of the word is clear) for guessing, don't leave any question blank. (In some tests, you lose double credit for any

error. These tests, though, are rare, and you are usually advised, in advance, that you should not guess. If you are not told "Don't guess because you will lose credit for guessing," go ahead and take a chance.) Actually, a guess is based, as a general rule, on something you know. You may not even be aware of the fact that you know it, for the material is often in your subconscious mind.

6. If the answer required is an essay, write as much as you can—but keep within the time limit. Never finish an exam with essays before the time is up. Work for every second you have. Make yourself add to what you have already written.

7. Prepare for exams by studying with a friend. Each of you ask the other questions. In this way, you are testing each other, and can often discover exactly in which areas you are not too well prepared.

Testing is part of our educational system, and, as such, our children need to be prepared for it. When you find youngsters who usually do poorly on tests, try to find out why. Is it because they cannot interpret the questions? In whichever area a child is deficient, try to work with him—so that he does not feel he will never improve or never do well on a test. He faces many of them in the 12 or more years he will be in school.

Teaching children social behavior in this changing world

Before you can teach children how other people get along in the world, you have to learn how they feel about themselves and others. One way to do this is through discussion; another is through role playing. Still a third is through a questionnaire. We will give you some of the items here, so that, should you wish to use this technique, you will be able to construct your own series of questions:

A questionnaire on social attitudes

1. If someone asked you to introduce yourself, what would you say, after you said your name?

2. How many brothers and sisters do you have? How old are they? How many live at home?

3. If you have a best friend, who is he or she?

4. If you have two best friends, who are they?

5. How many other friends do you have?

6. Some people are private persons, who have no close friends, or only one. They want to be that way. Some of them are quite famous. Are you a private person?

7. When you are with your friends, what do you like to do?

8. When you are by yourself, what do you enjoy doing most?

9. If you have to choose one activity, which would you choose—reading a book, playing jacks, playing ball, watching television, or having a discussion or talking with a number of your friends?

10. If you have to choose one activity, which would you choose—roller skating, riding a bicycle, listening to records, or baby sitting?

If you wish to give a questionnaire to your children, tell them that if they do not wish to fill it out they don't have to. It may be a painful experience for the "private people," but you will have observed this, and don't really need the questionnaire to ascertain it.

With this tool, you can easily learn a great deal about the children in your class. Usually your findings will bear out what you have observed, but not always. Don't be surprised if they differ. Let's look at the responses to these questions.

The answer to the first will usually be "I'm Peter Rabbit (not really, but Peter So-and-So). I go to P.S. #___ and I'm in class___." This, if the child identifies with his classmates, is comfortable in the school, and is able to verbalize well. If he can't write well, he may only add a word or two of explanation.

The second question gives you an idea of the family constellation. By studying it, you learn a bit about the youngsters' backgrounds. Sometimes, children in very large families are quiet because they are told to be "seen and not heard." Others try for an inordinate amount of attention in school because they do not get it at home.

Questions three through six help you to see which children have problems of a social nature. Number six is worded in the manner in which it is to avoid hurting the child who is not very social. But, once you are aware of it, and this almost always bears out your observations, you can help him.

Seven, eight, nine and ten really give you similar information, but in a different form. The real loner chooses to read or to listen to records; he selects activities which do not place him with people. Yet he needs this contact, needs to learn how to react to others, and can benefit immensely if you can help him to become more social.

What should be the extent of your work? You may decide to refer the child to the guidance counselor, if you feel the problem is one you cannot handle. On the other hand, you can devise a program to follow with this child—to give him individualized instruction in making friends. Here are some of the steps you might take:

1. Invite the child to have lunch with you. Talk with him about himself. In the course of the conversation, find out whether he has any friends, or not. Is he particularly shy, or, on the contrary, is he overbearing? Why would he not have friends? What is there about him which makes him a loner? In speaking with him, bring out the fact that friends listen to other people—that they are really interested in them, and that they show that interest. Also, that a person, in order to have friends, must be a friend. He must be willing to do things for others, and sometimes be willing to take the first step. The shy child rarely volunteers for anything. Try to make him see this. He stays away from team activities, for instance. Encourage him to join school, or other desirable, teams. If you can, get the idea across to him that he needs to communicate with his peers. Some children do not know how to engage in conversation, and you may even have to suggest topics he can discuss, such as class events. Be subtle, but try to get this idea across to him, and over lunch is a very good time to do so.

2. Establish committees of two or three children, and, if you have two loners, or two shy youngsters, place them together and give them a number of topics to discuss. Be sure each takes part in the discussion. Here is where individualized instruction can really help. Listen to the conversations, and try to observe wherein the trouble actually lies. Sometimes you will discover that one or both of the loners are self-centered or spoiled, and want their own ways all the time. If you can show them how impossible this is, and how detrimental, socially, you are able to accomplish a great deal.

3. Set up situations in the class where these loners will work

with other children, too, on a one-to-one basis. If they are able to handle it, have them tutor others. Watch the attitude, though, and if they behave in an overbearing fashion, point it out immediately.

4. Discuss the situation with the parents. Explain your efforts on the child's behalf, and, if you can, obtain their cooperation.

5. Take advantage of any trips on which you take the children to institute a closeness between the loners and other youngsters. The informality of the trip situation often makes this feasible.

6. By being a friend to this child, you enrich his or her life. One friend is better than none, and, even though you are the teacher, perhaps what this boy or girl needs desperately is a friend.

Giving children experiences in getting along together

We have mentioned committee work as an excellent means of giving children experiences in getting along together. You can also teach them to work to help others—really killing two birds with one stone—by initiating such projects as any of these:

1. A clothing drive for the needy.

2. A drive for canned food before Thanksgiving or Christmas.

3. A drive for toys before Christmas.

4. Raising money to support a child in an underdeveloped country, through an organization such as the Foster Parent Plan, 215 Park Avenue South, New York, N.Y. (It costs $16 per month.)

5. Participating in various Red Cross drives.

6. Helping any family which is struck by misfortune. We have known of various problems—such as fires destroying a family's entire home, including all of the children's clothing. Help is needed!

The concept of doing charitable work should be taught to the children when they are very young. It is the sort of activity which benefits everyone involved, and hurts no one.

As we mentioned in the chapter devoted to science, committees devoted to preserving our earth and conserving our resources are very important, and should not be overlooked as an excellent source of committee work.

Developing rapport with the disruptive child

If ever a child needs individualized instruction, particularly in regard to social behavior, it is the child who has not learned how to conduct himself in a classroom situation, and is constantly disruptive. How can you "get to" this child? First let us assure you—you can. He is far from unreachable, unless he is a really disturbed child—and even then this method will help you to "live" with him. However, if you expect to turn him into a paragon, forget it. He will not sprout wings, or become an angel. But he can be reached, and we can help him to improve his behavior.

First, arrange to speak to this child privately. Not while the class is in front of you, but alone. Perhaps over lunch, or even after school. It is important, though, that this be in a quiet place, and that you are not angry. If you are, the value is nil.

Then get the child to talk to you about himself. Ask about his family, but casually. Don't ever appear to be prying. "I've never met your family," you might say. "Tell me about them." Listen to what he tells you. You may find, as we often do, an unhappy situation. Make no comment. Then go on to ask, "Are you unhappy in this class?" If the child says yes, ask him why. Listen to his answer. If there is something you can do to improve the situation, tell him you will be very glad to do it. Assure the child you are his friend, as well as his teacher. Don't say it, though, if you don't mean it. There are some children to whom no teacher could say this, and if he is one, don't utter the words. But, if you can, then tell him this, and say, too, "I would like you to be happy and I want, very much, to help you to do your work. Do you think you can?" If the child says, "Yes," then say to him, "Will you promise me you'll try?" Go on to explain that you're asking him *to try*. This means that, later on, if he misbehaves, you can call him up to your desk and ask, "What's the matter? Is something wrong? You promised me you'd try. I know you want to keep your promise. Can I help you?"

Children are disruptive for many reasons. Sometimes, a child is upset by events at home, so much so that he comes into school ready to tear the place apart. Others are frustrated because they cannot read or do the work demanded of them. For whatever reason, and there can be any of dozens, every non-functioning child still needs your help and understanding. (You may wish to read *Discipline and the Disruptive Child,* Karlin and Berger, Parker Publishing Company, Inc., West Nyack, N.Y. 1972. In this book these problems, and possible solutions for handling them are discussed in detail.)

If you show a child you do understand, and you do want to help, he often responds positively and his behavior improves. It may be a slow process, but it can be a definite one. If he transgresses again, and he most probably will, again sit down and talk with him. Really listen to him. What is it that's bugging him? You may find it something as simple as the kids in the class teasing him, or as complex as a deep-seated behavioral disorder. When you find a serious situation or repeated incidents, get in touch with the guidance counselor, or with your supervisor.

Try, however, to establish good means of communication with the children. Some youngsters need someone to talk to, and have learned that they receive attention when they do something negative. It's sad, but true. Perhaps, if you can arrange to give these children some tasks to do for you on a daily basis, or a frequent one, they will assume the responsibility, and their behavior will improve. We have seen this work very effectively. "I need you to do this (and you state the specific task) for me. I'm counting on you." Then add, "If something is troubling you, talk with me about it. I am not sure I can help you with it, but I can try. And sometimes, if you talk about it, you'll feel better."

When a child has learning problems, it is up to you to work with him—toward a partial solution, if not a full one. If a child cannot read, you have already done a diagnostic test, and can show him that you are working on this. You can direct his efforts so that he sees he is getting somewhere. Make him see that he is making progress—and you will find his frustration will diminish.

Summary

Teaching consists of conveying to our children so many skills, so many concepts, so many facts that to try to include all of them is a bit like trying to count the grains of sand on some lovely beach. But we must select those aspects we feel are important and focus our attention on them. Surely, learning how to study and how to take tests are essentials. The methods we have outlined are not the only ones, but they are techniques youngsters have found to be effective. If you have your own method, which you wish to add or to substitute, do so, by all means. But if you haven't, expose your children to these. They need some education in these areas—areas which are often sadly neglected.

Most children learned social skills as they grew, but, for those who have not, this is a necessity. Individualizing your instruction, you can work with such youngsters, and really affect changes in their behavior which can make an important difference in their lives. To discover which children require such help, we have included a simple questionnaire which will usually reinforce what you have observed in your classroom. If a child needs assistance, a program is outlined which you may follow.

Children need experiences in getting along together. These can be structured at the same time that you are developing in them a desire to help other human beings less fortunate than themselves. Both aspects are extremely valuable.

The child who does not function well in your classroom may behave this way for any one of a number of reasons. For whatever reason, very often you can work with him. A series of procedures are listed which you may find helpful. They require you to work with him, and particularly to listen to him, on a one-to-one basis.

It is our belief that the real essence of education is teaching a child how to solve his problems, how to cope with his life. In the case of the child who is non-functioning, individualized instruction can be the break-through. You can make it possible for him to function in the academic society, which he must be in for most of his childhood.

Children respond to love and to sympathy almost every time. Of course, you will find those who are emotionally ill or frozen, and cannot. But even they will respond sometimes. One of the authors had the joy of having a very troubled young man, whom she had mentally nicknamed "The Great Stone Face," because he never seemed to smile or enjoy anything, bend over, and kiss her goodbye at graduation. This was before an audience of two thousand. He smiled, and whispered "Thanks a million." And, until that moment, she never knew she had reached him.

13

Evaluating your success
with individualized instruction

Every teacher should constantly evaluate his or her teaching. If you don't do this, how can you possibly tell if your pupils are really learning? One young teacher told of her experiences this way: "I would say to the children, during my first two months of teaching, after I had covered something, 'You understand, don't you?' They would nod their heads 'yes,' and I would continue with the lesson. I didn't give a test or a quiz until I had finished a unit which lasted about six weeks. Then I told the youngsters they would be getting this important test, and ordered, begged and pleaded with them to study. The highest mark in that test was 36. I cried and cried. I thought I was a failure. Fortunately, my buddy teacher asked me what was wrong. We discussed the situation. Her first comment was, 'But how could you have waited six weeks to find out if the children were learning what you were teaching them?' Then we went over the test. She asked me, 'Don't you think this is too difficult for them?' And when I read it carefully, I agreed—it was college level—and I was teaching seventh graders."

Evaluation should be a constant process

Constant evaluation is a necessity. You should not give long, involved unit tests every week, but you do need some criteria to be sure that you are reaching every child, and that, if you are not, you give individual attention to the children who need it.

How can you do this constant evaluation?

1. Give short quizzes. Multiple choice or completion questions are excellent for this purpose. Have the children mark one another's papers. Five to ten questions are adequate, and will give you an idea of whether the children are learning.

2. You need not take down every mark. Your youngsters will love it when you say, "This quiz doesn't count. It's for me—to see if you're learning what I'm teaching." This can be done occasionally.

3. Even more, they love to take a "test," and have you say, "I'll only count this if you get over 85. If not, I won't add it to your grades, or average it in." How can you do this? Simple. It just isn't averaged in. You will find that children will do approximately the same level of work throughout the year. Not averaging in some marks, in the long run, has little effect. Furthermore, this system inspires the children to try—because you say, "Here is a chance for you to really bring your average up." Your high ability students will get an abundance of 95's. Your mediocre students may pull themselves up, and sometimes even the less responsive children improve.

4. Toward the end of a unit of work, give a unit test to determine how much the children have learned. Use this test as an indication, too, of which pupils need more work in a specific area. Then, while the rest are completing the unit with more advanced material, you can reteach the basics to those boys or girls who missed them before.

5. Let us say that, if you give review notes, the children will know exactly what you expect them to know and can, consequently, study far more effectively. However, don't take every question directly from these notes. We suggested approximately 80 percent, but you may vary the number, depending upon the group of children you are teaching.

Pretesting before initiating individualized instruction

Many teachers have found the pretest very effective because it gives them a starting point. For instance, it is used very frequently in the teaching of spelling. If, however, most of the children know most of the words, what is the point of teaching them the words they already know? The same is true of any subject. If the boys and girls know the material, don't waste time on it. You can hold them responsible for it, but don't belabor it. If you do, the children often become bored. "We never learn anything new," some of them had been heard to comment, and when the situation was investigated, the remark was almost true. This particular class had had a very stimulating, effective teacher the year before, and she had covered much of the following year's curriculum. The next teacher was not aware of this, and did not heed the youngsters' complaints until this fact was brought to her attention by a supervisor. The group was a very bright group—and needed more advanced work as a result. It is poor policy to teach the next year's curriculum. Enrichment, in the form of related topics, or taking the current year's topics in far greater depth, is preferable.

Particularly in the teaching of the skill areas, the pretest can be used as your diagnostic test, as well. Think about how often youngsters are taught material they already know because the teacher is not aware of it. Not because they were formally taught it, as in the case above, but because they absorbed it along the way. Let us say you are teaching the class how to write a business letter. (Let us digress for a moment. This topic is a must, yet we have found an unbelievably large number of students unable to handle it, because they do not know the format.) You ask the class to write the business letter, and after they have written it, you review the details with them, while they go over their own papers, making corrections. If a child has made only one or two unimportant errors, why should he have to write another letter? Or perhaps just one, for practice, and to get it right, once and for all. Or you may decide to assign reading to him, suggesting that he select a book from the class library. Perhaps you think a report on careers related to the language arts would be more worthwhile. (Editing, publishing, journalism, drama, acting, directing, the communications media are examples of such careers.) Have him work on any project which is associated with the subject you are teaching. In this case it is English. This will be more valuable to him than rewriting a letter again and again—when he did it satisfactorily the first or second time.

Activities need not be called "pretests" to function as such. The letter-writing, above, is an example of this. Do not require a child to spend any more time on a topic than is needed—don't waste his time—it's far too precious. However, don't accept sloppy work, either. This is your chance to say, "If you do this piece of work well, you can go on to the next assignment. If you are careless, you waste your own time—and effort."

End of unit tests are diagnostic tests, too

You have almost finished a unit (about a week to ten days before) and are testing the class on it. Every child will not have learned everything you have covered. However, you should decide on the following:

1. Which basic concepts should every child know?
2. Which facts should every child know?
3. Which concepts and facts should the average student know? (This is the child who usually gets between 65 percent and 80 percent.)
4. Which material should the students who get from 80 percent to 90 percent know?
5. Which material should the very bright children have learned?

Then, when the papers are marked, you have criteria. If the children have achieved as well, or better, than you expect, they can go on to complete the unit. If they have not, then you should review the papers to determine which areas need to be retaught, and to which children. This reteaching can be done by some of the youngsters, if necessary, or you can teach groups yourself. But you cannot teach everything to everyone, so it is essential you decide beforehand, and write your questions with this idea in mind. There should be some material that you expect only the brightest youngsters to learn. You will find a number of youngsters who will surprise you, and who will move into higher levels—if you are motivating them, and if they have become involved in what you are teaching.

Varying and individualizing the types of tests you give—oral, open book, essay and short-answer

You can add variety to your lessons by changing the types of tests you give. Not only that, but, as you will see, the test itself can be a teaching tool.

In oral testing, you may ask a child to cover a certain topic by telling you all he knows about it. The topic should, of course, be very limited. If the youngster is able to think on his feet, this can be a very valuable experience for him. Some may welcome it. Others will be too nervous. Even if you wish to use this, don't force it on any youngster, because it could possibly have a negative effect.

Open book tests are generally more popular. These are very good if you wish to test interpretation and critical thinking. You might, for example, make a statement, and then ask the children to prove it right or wrong. In their proof, they have to find facts which back up their opinions. "The moon is made of green cheese," you say to them. Everyone laughs. But then they have to find facts. Of course their textbooks will not have a statement to the effect that the moon isn't made of green cheese, but they will be able to find indications of what it is actually made of. This is an oversimplification, of course, but it gives you an idea of how interesting questions may be developed.

Don't use this technique just to have the children find facts—unless fact-finding is the skill you are teaching them. But it is no great feat to find the capital of Minnesota is St. Paul, in an atlas or a geography text. "Why are Minneapolis and St. Paul called the 'twin cities,' " is better, and still better is "Why were these cities built so close together?"

Essay questions are used to determine whether a child can think through an answer to a problem. Most often, they call for one of the following:

1. A list of factors:

"List the reasons why the ocean will be needed to supply more of the food for the population of the world."

2. A comparison:

"How is the continent of Antarctica similar to other continents? How is it different?"

3. An explanation:

"Why does the disappearance of the dinosaurs present a mystery to scientists?"

"How does a windmill operate? Why do we see so few in operation today?"

4. A procedure:

"How would you select a man to run for the Presidency of the United States?"

"How did the pioneers bake their bread? How do we bake it today?"

5. An interpretation;

"Consult the graph on page X, and based on it, predict how many people there will be on the earth by the year 2020."

The essay requires a more sustained effort than short-answer questions. The child must read it, think about it, understand what is being asked of him, and work out an answer to it. It can reveal whether or not he grasps a concept. Since it is encountered so often as the child advances academically, we believe it must be included in our teaching program as early as possible. *If a child cannot read the question, have him read it aloud with you.*

Short-answer questions are basic to the teaching of most subjects. They reveal a child's mastery of certain information. Remember, too, that they indicate his ability to read, and, as with the essay, if a youngster is handicapped in this regard, he is penalized for not knowing information which he very well may know—but does not realize is being requested.

You have at your disposal a variety of form these questions may take.

1. Multiple choice
2. Completion
3. True-false
4. True-false-change (For example, you instruct the children to write the word "true" if a question is correct. If it is false, they are to change the word underlined, to make the statement true. For example, *"Boston* is the capital of the United States." The statement is false. To make it true, the child must cross out the word Boston and must write "Washington, D.C." in its place.)
5. Matching, with an even number of items in both columns.
6. Matching, with an uneven number of items in both columns.

Short-answer questions are used by many teachers, very frequently, in pretesting and in diagnostic testing. They are also used in programmed learning.

By constantly changing the type of question you ask, you keep the youngsters on their toes, intellectually speaking. You demand more concentration, and you help them to develop a familiarity with tests, which usually results in improvement in subsequent examinations.

Teaching every child the technique for answering essay questions

The ability to answer an essay question is absolutely essential—if a child is to succeed academically, and yet we have seen many, many children reach the seventh or eighth grade without ever having been taught how to do so.

We suggest you teach every child how to handle an essay question. Perhaps these ideas will be of help: Instruct the youngsters to:

1. Analyze the question. What, specifically, is being asked for? It may help you to underline these key words.

2. What other factors have to be taken into consideration to answer this question?

3. How many points does the answer have to have? If this is not stated in the question, give as many as possible.

4. If you can think of anything related to the answer to add, and have the time, add it. You may receive credit. You can't lose any.

5. After you have written your answer, read it over again carefully. Are you sure you are expressing the ideas you are trying to get across to the person reading your answer? *Did you answer the question?*

With these steps in mind, give your children several essays to answer—over a period of about a week. Review these. You will easily find those youngsters who need extra assistance in essay answering.

If a child has not learned how to write a sentence correctly, this is an excellent time to teach it to him. "Each thought, in answering an essay, should be in a sentence of its own, since this makes the answer simpler to mark," you tell him. Perhaps in this situation, in relation to test taking, it will penetrate.

Allowing the class to grade its own tests

Marking tests can take up an inordinate amount of your time. You can save this, for the most part, and, at the same time, make maximum use of your tests—both pretests and post-tests by having the class mark them. We have worked out this system, and found it very successful.

1. Have the children write with ballpoint pens when they take the test.

2. When the test is over, have them put the ball point pens away.

3. Collect the papers, and redistribute them, so that the children do not grade papers of youngsters sitting near them.

4. Now, have the children take out pencils, and use only pencil to grade the papers.

5. Have the child correcting the paper write the words "Corrected by___" and sign his name at the end of the paper.

6. Write the point value of each answer on the board before you give the correct answer.

7. If an answer is correct, have the person marking the paper leave it alone, or place a small check next to it.

8. If an answer is wrong, have the marker indicate "Minus three" (-3) next to it. (Or whatever the question is worth.)

9. At the end of a section, have the person marking the paper add up all of the minuses, and write the total numbers of minuses (let us say there were four questions, each worth -3. Therefore the person would write -12 in the margin.) Then, when all of the sections have been marked, these sums are added together, and subtracted from 100.

10. To give partial credit, tell the youngsters exactly how many points to deduct. It is the simplest way to handle this, we have found from experience.

11. You can even have the youngsters mark essays—if you know exactly how much credit you are giving for each point which should be included in the answer.

This aspect of grading is, of course, more complex than the

short-answer part. Therefore, if you wish, you can do this part yourself. However, it really is not necessary, and it is actually an excellent learning experience for the children. When you compose your test, think in terms of breaking down the essay for grading purposes. For example, "List the conditions necessary for erosion to occur." You have decided there are four points which should be given in the answer. Therefore, each has equal value, when the essay is marked. If an unexpected response is given, the youngster marking the paper will question you, and you make your decision at that time.

12. In going over the questions, both the short-answer and the essays, have the children give the correct answers. This creates an air of excitement, and is also a learning experience. A high school student was heard to say, "I never, in my whole life, will forget that the complexion of the Black Knight (in *Ivanhoe*) was swarthy. I got it wrong on the test, and then I had to get it wrong while we were going over the papers. Out loud!" That was some thirty years ago, and so far, she hasn't forgotten.

13. You can encourage this feeling of excitement by giving partial credit, or by asking the class if partial credit should be given for a particular answer, and by discussing each answer as it is given. You will find the children very responsive.

14. After the papers are marked, return them to their owners and review them again. Then comes the fun! "I got this right, but I was marked wrong. I wuz robbed!" is inevitable. And it does happen often. Furthermore, children often add or subtract incorrectly. And the essays are open to negotiation. But the children do use their powers of concentration and of persuasion, and they do learn from this marking process. They learn, too, we have discovered, how to write a better answer to an essay question— because they see many examples of what is expected of them.

Reviewing the test results and using them for individualization

As we have shown, this unit test indicates which areas must be retaught to which children. Since you have already decided which specific areas everyone should have mastered, you begin with those the youngsters haven't learned successfully. Your questions will point it up almost automatically. If any one child, or several children, need additional work on these topics, you can teach it to them, while the rest of the class is completing the unit. Next go on to the average students. Reteach any material they should have mastered, but didn't. In both cases, give homework, some form of assignment, to reinforce the teaching you did in class.

If you have the time, work, too, with the better students. Instead of having them cover new work, give them the responsibility of learning what they missed. You may assign additional reading on the subject to them, if you wish, and ask them to summarize what they have read. You may have the children work together on this type of assignment.

You may discover, in reviewing the test, that many children did poorly on the same topic. Don't be disturbed. Reteach it—but handle it differently. Try to approach it from another angle. You might ask one of the brighter pupils to reteach it. Sometimes, it needs a different slant to get across. Usually, most of your children will understand what you are teaching. Rarely will you have to reteach anything to the entire class. However, if you must, don't let this disturb you.

But, if you find that this situation does come up repeatedly, you are teaching above the children's level. Don't let it "throw you." Review your work. Perhaps the vocabulary is too difficult. Possibly the children don't have the background to understand what you are teaching. Perchance they have erroneous ideas. For whatever reason, don't become discouraged. Just simplify your material, and see what happens. It is so easy for young teachers, just out of college, to expect too much from their children. The inexperienced teacher may credit the youngsters with more ability than they actually have.

Building a success pattern with testing

By using tests, you can help each child to build a success pattern. But first, why is this worthwhile? Why should you seek to do this? "Aren't the grades the child gets just an indication of his work and his ability?" you ask.

There are children, in our schools, and possibly in your class, who have known so little success in school that they are almost conditioned to fail. Consciously or unconsciously, they feel they haven't a chance in the world to do better—so they refuse to try. They will not put themselves into that failure situation again. Oh, they do fail, but they have removed themselves. To us it may appear, "Joey couldn't care less." Perhaps by now it's almost true. But, down deep, no child wants to fail—and certainly not all of the time. You can reach this child—and his more capable classmates—if you make a conscious effort to do so. One way is by building a success pattern.

Here are some steps to take. Of course you may vary them to suit your class.

1. Tell the children you are sure they are all going to do well. Some may look at you rather skeptically. Assure them.

2. Give the children the material from which the test questions will be taken, as has been outlined previously.

3. Write as many tests as you need—this may be five or six. Then give each child his own individual test. For slower students, make the test so simple that they will do well. They may realize it, but *show* them the test counts by putting the grade in your marking book.

4. Have each child make a graph showing his progress.

5. After you have given a test, graded it in class, gone over the errors, and retaught the material, give the same test over again to those children who did poorly. Call it a RETEST. Most of the time the children will have learned the material the second time around, if not the first. Count the result of this retest, and have the child place it on the graph, too.

6. Discuss with the slower learner the fact that he has the ability to learn. Work on this with him. Most slow learners aren't really slow. They often have reading problems. You can get around that by reading the questions to the child, if the test is in a subject other than reading.

7. Give short quizzes, even twice a week. Your children will probably do better in these, because they have just covered the material recently.

8. If there is a wide variation of ability in your class, develop a number of unit tests, rather than just one. Suit them to the child, so that he is not overwhelmed.

When a child who has not passed a test for a very long time does so, you can chalk up one point for him, and for yourself. If he passes several, you will feel his attitude changing. We have found that children who present very severe discipline problems are often helped greatly by this approach. *They want, very desperately, to do well.* One boy in this category, after one particular test, came up to ask "Can I take this home, to show to my mother? I'll bring it back. I never did this good before." That was the teacher's reward for having sat up the night before composing six different tests for her class.

9. An excellent way to show each child's progress is to keep a folder of his or her work. Obtain one large folder (or envelope) for each child from the stockroom. Place his name prominently on it. Tell the youngsters you are keeping a file of their work, and that, of course, they will want it to contain only the very best work they can do. Allow them to keep in it papers they have corrected as well as tests which were graded by the teacher.

Keep a file of your tests

No teacher ever teaches any class exactly the same way she taught another. But she does cover, very often, the same material. Therefore, while she may not want to use any previous test, in toto, she can use parts of it. When you are writing a number of tests, keep them in a looseleaf book, with notations and dates.

In fact, never, never discard your plans, your tests, or any materials you develop. You will find they are very valuable to you—and to other teachers, too, if you care to share them.

Designing good questions can be a chore. Why do it repeatedly? Instead find your previous year's work, and refer to it for assistance.

You may have help from an unexpected source. Ask your children to make up questions, which you can then use on the review sheets. This is a very valid assignment; since it teaches the selection of the main idea of a lesson, it takes into consideration important facts, and the children can be taught to work out questions which deal with concepts, as well.

You may, at times, use questions from the text. The authors have devoted time and energy to developing them, and again, while all may not be applicable, some of them are. Check the

Teacher's Guide to the particular text you are using, for further ideas.

Evaluating individual growth in social behavior

Testing is a relatively simple way to evaluate certain aspects of your program. Evaluating the children's growth in other areas is far more difficult because you will have to trust to your observations. Much of this evaluation you will be doing constantly.

1. Observation.

You have set up objectives, for yourself, in regard to the development of social attitudes. Have the youngsters learned to work well in committees? Are they able to cooperate as a whole group?

Have the children befriended the loner? Has he or she learned how to be a friend?

Have the children been open-minded to opinions other than their own? Can they air their views, as well?

Have ideas of consideration of others really penetrated?

We are dealing with many intangibles here, but they are more important than facts, in terms of the development of the whole human being. With these questions in mind, review your class and their actions. Where do they still need help, and where have they been successful? As teachers become involved in curriculum, and in working with the individual child to assist him with his learning problems, or to enrich him, it is easy to let these objectives be forgotten. Yet they are the essence of education.

2. "Rap sessions" with small groups of children.

Another device you may use to evaluate your program is to hold "rap sessions" with your students. These are informal group discussions, when others are not around, during which the children can really talk about what is bothering them. These sessions often reveal things which are troubling the youngsters, but which they have been unable to discuss.

3. One-to-one talks.

By talking with children, on a one-to-one basis, how can you discern their growth in social behavior? For example, you can set up a hypothetical situation—describe it to the youngster—and then have him tell you his reactions. From these, you can see if he has learned more about getting along with others.

For instance, you say to a child, "Bobby, let's imagine you are in the lunchroom. A boy pushes you. You don't know whether it was accidental or not. What would you do? The boy is a little smaller than you. How would you handle the situation?"

4. Consulting the parents.

When a child has had difficulty in social situations, you may wish to discuss the matter with his parents to see if they have seen any improvement in his behavior at home. This is very important—if you have been working with him on social behavior. Furthermore, it is a way of informing the parents that you have been doing this individualized instruction with their child. One parent, when questioned, told the teacher, "So that's why he's changing. We noticed it, but we almost couldn't believe it. How can we ever thank you?"

Summary

Individualized instruction, as with any teaching technique you may use, should be evaluated constantly, in order for you to be able to tell if you are really reaching your children—if the method is proving to be effective.

You can judge how well your children are learning skills or curricular material by testing. Pretests are valuable to determine what information a child already has and, therefore, does not have to be taught again. End-of-unit tests serve both as reviews and as diagnostic tools, indicating to you which material must be retaught—and to which children.

Vary the type of questions you ask. You should include oral questions, open-book questions, essays, and of course, short-answer questions. Every child should be taught how to answer essay questions because he will most probably encounter them throughout his academic career. Your children can grade the test papers of other youngsters in their class, thereby reviewing the material, and at the same time, saving you a great deal of work.

Never, never give a test and neglect to mark it.

Never, never give a test, grade it, and forget it. Tests have far too much value as diagnostic tools to ignore them.

Tests may be used to help each child to build a success pattern. This is essential for those children who have had many negative learning experiences, in school, and who have, as a result, developed poor self-images.

In addition to evaluating your pupils' growth in academic areas, you should also check to see if your individualized instruction has helped them in social behavior as well. You may do this by observation, by "rap sessions" with small groups, by one-to-one talks, and by consulting with the child's parents.

A continuous program of individual and class evaluation will help to make your individualized instruction effective, as far as your children are concerned, and satisfying and rewarding for you.

Conclusion

We have described various techniques for the individualization of instruction in many subject areas. This does not imply that you must do so in every different subject you teach. We suggest, however, that you do use it first in reading and then in arithmetic, because it will help you to reach those children who are having difficulty, and also those who are in need of enrichment.

To individualize instruction, you must first diagnose. We have outlined simple, effective methods to do so. Without diagnosing, how can you possibly know wherein a child's problems lie? You can almost map his progress, and just as you would need a map if you were to explore terrain unknown to you, so you need diagnosis to clarify the terrain called reading in the child's mind. The same crying need for diagnosis is present when you are teaching arithmetic, or mathematics. Language arts, too, is concerned in some respects with skills, and diagnosis is needed in that area, as well.

In the other curriculum areas, individualized instruction is effective, but not as essential. However, when it comes to personality and social adjustment, one-to-one teaching can have a tremendous effect on a youngster who has problems. This is real teaching, which can help the child through his entire life. We refer to such aspects as working with others, making friends, or learning to compromise.

We firmly believe that individualized instruction should be

designed primarily for the most needy of our children—those who particularly need intellectual and spiritual guidance. It is a boon to the slow child, the borderline child, the hostile child, the sadistic child, the child with problems at home, the loner, the hypersensitive child, the child with a deep sense of intellectual insecurity ("Teacher, I can't!"), the foreign child who cannot speak the language, the child with physical or mental health problems, the moody child, the unhappy child, the child who cannot concentrate, the neurotic child, the attention-seeker (Give him some attention, by all means!), the lazy child, the bigoted child, and the unloved child. In the one-to-one relationship, let us work with all of these children, remembering always that the greatest—the greatest of all great teachers is love.

Index

A

Abstractions, drawing and painting,
76
Alcohol, 182
Anti-social tendencies in children:
develop conscience to counteract, 31, 32
provide healthful adventure to
counteract, 33
Arithmetic, 135-148
combat carelessness, 141, 142
curriculum, 138-141
number relationships, 140
practice, 140
"Puzzles," 140
work sheets, 140
diagnosis, 136-138
discovering inadequacies, 137,
138
testing, 136, 137
enrichment, 141, 145
games, 146, 147
laboratory, 147, 148
mathematical vocabulary, 144,
145
multiplication, 135, 136
problem solving, 142, 143
skills for success, 143, 144 (see
also Individualized instruction)
Autobiography, child's:
biography as example, 34
encourage writing, 34
questions to ask, 34, 35
read excerpts from life of famous person, 34

B

Behavior skills (see Skills)
Building positive self-image (see
Psychological needs)

C

Capitalization (see Language arts)
Career education (see Science)
Children teaching other children,
74
Child's needs:
academic, 7, 8
as a human being, 8
Cigarette smoking, 182, 183
Compound words (see Words)
Comprehension (see Reading comprehension)
Condition children to complete
work, 29
Condition children to succeed, 29,
30
Contractions (see Words)
Conventional lesson plan (see
Lesson plan, conventional)
Creating time for individualized
instruction (see Establishing
routines)
Creativity opportunities, 185-200
avoid negative criticism, 192,
193
helping reluctant child, 191, 192
in art, 186, 187, 188, 190, 193
in art appreciation, 195, 196
in home economics, 188, 189,
190, 193, 194
in industrial arts, 188, 189
in music, 188, 189, 190, 194,
195
in music appreciation, 195, 196
new ideas, 188, 189, 190
sincere encouragement, methods,
193, 194
sports, 189, 195
teaching as art, 197-199
check results, 199

Creativity opportunities *(cont.)*
  teaching as art *(cont.)*
    even if "untalented," 197
    flexibility, 198, 199
    have materials available, 198
    instructions for students, 197,
      198
    motivate children, 197
    project sources, 199
    timing, 198
  using notebook to encourage, 25
Current events *(see* Social studies)

D

Debates (panel discussions) *(see*
  Social studies)
Determining child's needs, 21-24
  (see also Individualized
  instruction)
Diagnose, to find needs, 7
Diagnosis, basis of individualized
  instruction, 90
Diagnostic testing for individualized
  instruction *(see* Testing,
  diagnostic)
Diagnostic tests, essential to teaching reading, 90
Discipline and the Disruptive Child
  (publication), 213

E

Ecology (environment) *(see* Science)
English Language Arts (publication),
  111
Enrichment *(see* Arithmetic; Language arts)
Establishing routines, 64-74
  effect on creativity, 64, 65
  entering classroom, 66
    dismissal, 66
    fire drill, 66
    lining up, 66
    partners, 66
    rules for, 66
  hang up clothing, 68
  how to approach, 64, 78
  keeping classroom clean, 68, 69
    basket monitor, 68
    desk inspection, 68
    putting supplies away, 69
    select housekeepers, 68
  key to individualizing, 65

Establishing routines *(cont.)*
  seating, 67, 68
    apathetic child, 67
    chart, 67
    class host or hostess, 68
    health problem, 67
    plant monitor, 68
  step by step, 65
  timesavers, 71, 72
  to suit children, 65
Evaluate teaching, 215-230
  constantly, 215, 216
    review notes, 216
    short quizzes, 216
    "test," 216
    unit tests, 216
  pretesting, 216-218
    in skill areas, 217
    letter-writing, 217, 218
  social behavior, 227, 228 *(see
    also* Skills, behavior)
    consult parents, 228
    observation, 227
    one-to-one talks, 227, 228
    "rap sessions," 227
  tests, 216-228
    criteria after marking, 218
    end of unit, 218
    individual folders, 226
    individual tests, 225
    progress graph, 225
    reassurances, 225
    reference file, 226
    retest, 225
    reviewing results, 223, 224
    self-grading by class, 222, 223
    sources of questions, 226,
      227
    steps, 225
    tests to build success pattern,
      224-226
  varying, 219-222
    essay, 219-222
    open book, 219
    oral, 219
    short-answer, 220, 221

F

Field day, 73
Fire drill, dismissal as rehearsal, 66
  (see also Self-control)

Flash cards (*see* Lesson planning sample)

G

Geography (*see* Social studies)
Goals, establishing in individualized instruction, 30-36
   communication, 30
   counteracting anti-social tendencies, 32 (*see also* Stealing by children)
   create desire to learn, 31
   detect personality problems, 33
   detect physical problems, 33
   develop responsibility to others, 31
   function as group members, 30, 31
   one-to-one relationship with child, 31-33
   reading comprehension, 31
   teach children good manners, 33
Grades as rewards, 83
Grammar (*see* Language arts)
Grouping children by needs, 26, 27

H

Handwriting (*see* Language arts)
History (*see* Social studies)

I

Individualized instruction:
   based on understanding needs, 29
   begin by getting to know your children, 34-36
   build a success pattern, 76, 77 (*see also* Test)
      bonus academic assignments, 77
      choice of activities, 77
      kinds of assignments, 76
   children mark own papers, 73
   determining child's needs, 21-24
   diagnosis to determine child's needs, 18
   diagnostic testing as basic tool, 22
   explaining to child, 72, 73
   for average child, 19
   for bright child, 18-20

Individualized instruction *(cont.)*
   group work, 74-76
   importance in primary grades, 17, 18
   individual goals for children, 34-36 (*see also* Goals)
   in motivating children to learn, 27
   key factors, 17, 18
   not solely for slow learner, 19
   parents' cooperation, 73
   research projects, 74-76
   self-control essential, 79-89
   skills, 20, 21
      arithmetic, 20 (*see also* Arithmetic)
      assign priorities, 22
      diagnostic testing to evaluate, 21
      in science, 21
      in social studies, 21
      lacking in bright children, 20, 21
      penmanship, 25
      reading, 21, 23
      social behavior, 21
      written English, 20
   structuring class for, 8
   subject area, 20
   teaching emphasis, 8
   to teach every child, 18-20
   unity stressed, 72
Individualized responsibility (*see* Responsibility individualized)
Inflectional endings (*see* Words)

K

Key to individualizing, 65

L

Language arts skills, 110-134
   capitalization, 115-117, 127-131
   class production, 120-122
   communication areas, 110
   enrichment, 132, 133
      editing class newspaper, 133
      lesson preparation, 133
      reading, 132, 133
      research, 133
   establishing goals, 110

Language arts
  grammar, 113-115, 127-131
    fifth year, 114, 115
    first year, 114
    fourth year, 114
    second year, 114
    sixth year, 115
    third year, 114
  handwriting, 127-134
    teaching in lower grades, 127-
      131
  learning listening, 126, 127
  learning verbal expression, 125,
    126 (*see also* Spoken
    language)
  parental aid, 123
  punctuation, 115, 117, 127-131
  related careers, 217
  sentence structuring, 123
  spelling, 115-117
    bees, 117
    check progress, 117
    diagnostic testing, 116
    pretest, 116
  spoken language, 110-112
    goals, 112
    reaching goals, 113
    skills to teach, 111
    usage, 111, 112
  vocabulary expansion, 123, 124
  vocabulary games, 124, 125
  work on specific skills, 122
  written language, 118-122
    compositions, 118
    diagnostic tests, 118
    individualizing, 119-122
    portfolio, 120
    subject matter, 118, 119, 120
Lesson plan, conventional, 36, 37
  parts, 36, 37
    aim (example), 36
    concepts (example), 37
    homework suggestions, 37
    individualize, 37
    materials, 37
    motivate, how to (example),
      36
    questioning, 37
Lesson planning:
  advice from colleagues, 45
  based on diagnosis, 8

Lesson planning *(cont.)*
  bright child as teacher, 45
  check child's understanding, 45
  consider different rates of learn-
    ing, 44
  flexibility, 45
    examples, 45
  individualized, 8
    in skills area, 8
  keeping records, 38, 39, 46
  objectives, discuss with class, 45
  traditional, 8
    new material for entire class,
      8
  units, 37-47
    contract to individualize in-
      struction, 27
    definition, 37
    examples of stimulating
      child's interest, 38
    for easier individualization,
      37, 38
    lessons included, 37
    objectives for each, 39
    range of assignments, 38
    skill development linked, 37
    textbook in dividing curricu-
      lum, 37
  unit sample:

    application in other subjects,
      42
    capital letter, 41, 43
    flash cards to teach word
      recognition, 42
    games with words, 42, 43
    objectives, 40-42
    phonic elements, 41
    punctuation, 41, 43
    questions, 40
    salient words, 40
    second grades, 39-42
    spelling, 41
    teaching sentence structure,
      42, 43
    understanding new words, 42
    understanding simple sentence,
      41
    word building, 41
    word recognition, 41
    writing simple sentences, 41

Lesson planning *(cont.)*
  vary teaching approaches, 44,
    45
  when results unsatisfactory, 44,
    45
Lesson plans:
  as reminders for other units, 46
  use for future reference, 46
Library:
  classroom, 36
    monitors, 36
    screen comic books, 36
    selection sources, 36
    sports magazines, 36

M

Motivating children, 24-29 (*see also*
    Lesson plan, conventional)
  build on success, 28
  by encouraging success, 27
  discuss topics with each child,
    27, 28
  display completed project, 28
  pictures, use of, 28
  projects for higher grades, 28
  projects for young children, 28
  word cards, 29
Multiplication (*see* Arithmetic)

N

Narcotics (*see* Survival lessons)

P

Parties; as rewards, 83 (*see also*
    Psychological needs)
Penalties (*see* Self-control)
Penmanship training necessary in
    any subject, 25 (*see also*
    Handwriting)
Phonetic analysis (*see* Reading,
    word learning)
Prefixes (*see* Words)
Pretesting (*see* Evaluate teaching)
Projects for higher grades, 28
Projects for young children, 27
Psychological needs, 48-63
  basics, 48
  building positive self-image, 48-
    61

Psychological needs *(cont.)*
  building self-image *(cont.)*
    assembly programs, 49
    athletics, 49
    beautify classroom, 52
    by making child responsible,
      50, 51
    care of classroom details, 49
    commendation cards, 58
    commendation letters, 58, 59
    defeat defeatist attitude, 59,
      61
    developing self-pride, 52, 53
    example, fifth graders' books,
      52
    exhibit work, 49
    grades as rewards, 56
    graph to measure individual
      progress, 51
    moody child, 62
    negative influences, 50
    neurotic child, 62
    obese child, 61, 62
    parties as rewards, 54-57
    party occasions, 56, 57
    responsibility for living things,
      50, 51, 53, 54 (*see also*
      Science)
    reward accomplishment, 54-
      59
    sick child, 61, 62
    singing, 49
    teaching by some children, 49
    trips as rewards, 57, 58
  experiencing failure, 48, 49
  measuring, 48-63
    observe child's appearance, 49
    observe child's work, 49
Punctuation (*see* Language arts)

R

Reading, 90-109
  aloud, 105, 106
  assignments to raise achievement
    level, 105, 106
  avoid boredom, 106-108
    making pleasurable, 107, 108
    races, 108
  children teaching other children,
    104, 105 (*see also* Psycho-
    logical needs)

Reading *(cont.)*
  comprehension, 102-104 (*see also* Goals; Skills)
    critical thinking, 103, 104
    diagnose progress, 93-95
    interpreting meanings, 102, 103
    literal, 102
    sample paragraph, 93, 94
    sample questions, 94
    standardized tests, 94, 95
    test for, 90, 91
  "contracts," 105, 106
  definition, 96
  diagnosis essential, 90
    oral test, 90, 95
    preparing study material, 96
    questions to ask, 91
    vocabulary development, 91-93
    vocabulary testing in reverse, 93
  grouping, 104, 105
  in class, 106
  individually, 104-105
  learning meaning, 95, 96
    mental pictures, 96
    troublesome "simple" words, 96
  teaching individualized, 90-109 (*see also* Individualized instruction)
  word learning, 96-102
    antonyms, recognition of, 102
    configuration clues, 96, 97
    contextual clues, 101, 102
    discerning meanings, 102
    discriminating between sounds, 98
    initial consonants, 99
    phonetic analysis, 98-100
    phonic games, 99, 100
    sample work sheet, 98, 99
    spoken language, 98 (*see also* Language arts)
    standardized tests, 94, 95
    synonyms, recognition of, 102
    teachers' guides, 98
    use of magazines, 99

Reading *(cont.)*
  word learning *(cont.)*
    use of newspaper, 99
    work sheets for each sound, 99, 100
    written language, 98 (*see also* Language arts)
  word recognition, 95
Regulations:
  handbook as project, 82, 83
    obtain class set, 82
  school, 82, 83 (*see also* Self-control, rules)
Responsibility individualized, 69-72
  dividing classroom work, 85
  examples, 70, 71
  getting it to function, 71
  monitorial tasks, 69
  reducing hostility, 69
  rules for, 69, 70
  self-confidence nourished, 70
  threat of removal, 70
Responsibilities of learning, 51
Rewards (*see* Self-control)
Run-on sentences, 7, 21, 22

S

Science, 167-184
  career education, 181
  curriculum individualized, 174-179
    contract examples, 175, 176
    contracts, 174-176
    grouping, 174, 179
    how to work with each child, 178, 179
    major projects, 177-179
    match texts to child, 177
    prehistoric dioramas, 178
    suggested topics, 178, 179
    weather topics, 178
  ecology (environment), 179, 180
  experiments, 170-173
    additional work, 172
    by child on himself, 172, 173
    chemicals, 172
    diagrams, 171
    for each child, 170-173
    how to proceed, 170
    notebook, 170, 171

Science *(cont.)*
  experiments *(cont.)*
    points to remember, 170-172
    safety rules, 172
    sources, 172
    use a control, 170
  for poor reader, 198
  questions involved, 167-170
    examples, 168-170
  responsibility for living things,
    180, 181
  restoring intellectual curiosity,
    167
  scientific method, 173, 174
    elements, 173
    examples, 173, 174
  survival lessons, 182, 183
  trips, 164
Scientific method *(see* Science)
Second grade sample unit *(see*
  Lesson planning)
Self-control:
  as asset, 88, 89
  basic fact of survival, 88
  class officers, elect, 85, 86
    train for fire drills, 86
  class teams, 85
  leadership training, 86
  penalties, 84, 85
    how to be fair, 84
  rewards, 83
  rule-making an occasion, 80
    avoid hostility, 80, 81 *(see*
      also Responsibility
      individualized)
    consider necessary areas, 80
    distribute copies, 81
    understanding laws, 81
    voting, 81
  rules children establish, 79-81
  teaching, 79-89 *(see also* Indiv-
    idualized instruction)
  working with problem children,
    86, 87
Self-esteem (positive self-image)
  (see Psychological needs)
Self-expression *(see* Creativity
  opportunities)
Sentence structuring *(see* Language
  arts)

Skills, behavior, 207-213
  committee work, 210
  disruptive child, 211, 212
  questionnaire analysis, 208, 209
  social attitudes questionnaire,
    207, 208
  steps to helping loner, 209, 210
  work-study, 201-208
    encourage use of methods,
      205
    how-to guide, 203, 204
    how to study, 202-206
    learn from text, 205
    review methods, 205
    to take tests, 206-208
    techniques for teaching, 202,
      203
Social studies, 149-166
  attitudes, 157, 158
  committee work, 161-163
    determine resources, 162
    dioramas, 163
    reports, 163
  curriculum, 152, 153
  debates (panel discussions), 156,
    157
  diagnosis, 150-152
    checklist, 150, 152
    observation important, 150
    social skills to consider, 152
  news reports, 161
  reading, 153-156
    comprehension, 153
    dictionary use, 154, 155
    essential, 153, 154
    vocabulary, 155, 156
    work-study skills, 154
  skills in living, 149, 150
  subjects included, 149
  teaching critical thinking, 159,
    160
  television guidance, 158, 159
  trips, 164, 165
    as motivation, 164
    bus setting ideal, 164
    for disadvantaged, 164, 165
Spelling *(see* Language arts)
Spoken language *(see* Reading, Word
  learning)
Stealing by children, 31, 32, 33
Stimuli outside classroom, 19, 20

*Successful Methods for Teaching
    the Slow Learner* (publica-
    tion), 19
Suffixes (*see* Words)
Survival lessons, 182 (*see* Sciences)

T

Teaching as art (*see* Creativity)
Teaching responsibility, 29
Teaching techniques:
    devices to use, 8
    evaluation, 8
    grouping children by needs, 8
    team teaching, 8
Team teaching, 76, 77 (*see also*
    Teaching techniques)
Television guidance (*see* Social
    studies)
Testing for evaluation of success, 8
Testing, diagnostic, 17-29 (*see also*
    Evaluate teaching; Individual-
    ized instruction; subjects, as
    Language arts)
    guidelines for developing tests,
        22, 23, 24
    informally, by examining written
        work, 24, 25
    results in conferences, 26
        enrichment material, 25
        exercises for tested areas, 25
        self-testing by child, 25, 26
        tutoring classmates, 26
    to evaluate skills, 21
    to learn child's topic deficiencies,
        29
    using results, 25, 26

Tests, varying (*see* Evaluate teach-
    ing)
Test to build success pattern, 224-
    226
Trips as educational experiences, 87
    (*see also* Psychological needs;
    Science)
    as rewards, 83
    for building teacher-student
        rapport, 87, 88

V

Vocabulary (*see* Language arts;
    Reading)
Vocabulary building (*see* Reading
    diagnosis; Word learning)

W

Word learning (*see* Reading)
Words:
    games, 101
    inflectional endings, 101
    parts, 100
    prefixes, 100
    roots, 101
    structural analysis, 100, 101
        compound words, 101
        contractions, 101
    suffixes, 101
        work sheets, 101
Work-study skills (*see* Social studies,
    reading; Skills)
Written language (*see* Reading;
    word learning; Individualized
    instruction)